REDISCOVERING *You*

A Guide to Life After Divorce

A hope*books COLLABORATION

Chapter One: Trusting the Journey Through the Unknown ©2025 Bridget Gengler

Chapter Two: Betrayal and Brokenness: Thriving Through the Pain ©2025 Julie Smith

Chapter Three: Weathering the Storm, Welcoming the Sun: From Uprooted to Rooted & Rising ©2025 Jennifer Burchill

Chapter Four: While Riding Through the Storm: Ways to Practice Self-Care During Divorce ©2025 Takhia Gaither

Chapter Five: The Journey of Lament in Divorce: Navigating Pain and Healing in Psalm 31 ©2025 Amy L. Boyd

Chapter Six: Hope in Every Season: Discovering Hope, Healing, and God's Faithfulness After the Storm ©2025 Angela King Bley

Chapter Seven: A New Plan A ©2025 Amber Brandt

Chapter Eight: Uncovering the Lies of Gaslighting: How Knowing the Truth Changes Everything ©2025 Ashley Boswell

Chapter Nine: Wholly Broken, Wholly Restored: How God Can Turn Our Pain into Purpose ©2025 Stephanie Lauren Jordan

Chapter Ten: Trust Fall: Trusting God That I Am Not Alone ©2025 Terra Richards

Published by hope*books

2217 Matthews Township Pkwy

Suite D302

Matthews, NC 28105

www.hopebooks.com

hope*books is a division of hope*media

Printed in the United States of America

All rights reserved. Without limiting the rights under copyrights reserved above, no part of this publication may be scanned, uploaded, reproduced, distributed, or transmitted in any form or by any means whatsoever without express prior written permission from both the author and publisher of this book—except in the case of brief quotations embodied in critical articles and reviews.

Thank you for supporting the author's rights.

First paperback edition.

Paperback ISBN: 979-8-89185-221-1

Hardcover ISBN: 979-8-89185-197-9

Ebook ISBN: 979-8-89185-198-6

Library of Congress Number: 2025937959

Scripture quotations marked (ESV) are taken from The ESV® Bible (The Holy Bible, English Standard Version®), © 2001 by Crossway, a publishing ministry of Good News Publishers. Used by permission. All rights reserved.

Scripture quotations marked (NLT) are taken from the Holy Bible, New Living Translation, copyright ©1996, 2004, 2015 by Tyndale House Foundation. Used by permission of Tyndale House Publishers, Carol Stream, Illinois 60188. All rights reserved.

Scripture referenced from The King James Version (KJV) are in the public domain and have been used in reverence to those who spent their lives translating the Word.

Scripture quotations marked (CSB) are taken from the Christian Standard Bible®, Copyright © 2017 by Holman Bible Publishers. Used by permission. Christian Standard Bible® and CSB® are federally registered trademarks of Holman Bible Publishers.

Scripture quotations marked (NKJV) are taken from the New King James Version®. Copyright © 1982 by Thomas Nelson. Used by permission. All rights reserved.

Table of Contents

Foreword vii

About the Chapters... ix

Chapter 1
Trusting the Journey Through the Unknown
By Bridget Gengler... 1

Chapter 2
Betrayal and Brokenness: Thriving Through the Pain
By Julie Smith 17

Chapter 3
Weathering the Storm, Welcoming the Sun:
From Uprooted to Rooted & Rising
By Jennifer Burchill... 27

Chapter 4
While Riding Through the Storm: Ways to
Practice Self-Care During Divorce
By Takhia Gaither.. 43

Chapter 5
The Journey of Lament in Divorce: Navigating Pain
and Healing in Psalm 31
By Amy L. Boyd.. 53

Chapter 6
Hope in Every Season: Discovering Hope, Healing,
and God's Faithfulness After the Storm
By Angela King Bley.. 73

Chapter 7
A New Plan A
By *Amber Brandt* 85

Chapter 8
Uncovering the Lies of Gaslighting: How Knowing
the Truth Changes Everything
By *Ashley Boswell* 99

Chapter 9
Wholly Broken, Wholly Restored: How God
Can Turn Our Pain into Purpose
By *Stephanie Lauren Jordan* 117

Chapter 10
Trust Fall: Trusting God That I Am Not Alone
By *Terra Richards* 129

About the Authors 139

Closing 150

Foreword

By Hope H. Dover

Divorce is not the story anyone plans for their life. No one walks down the aisle thinking the ending will include lawyers, custody schedules, or nights spent wondering how it all came undone. And yet, here you are with a broken heart, a changed last name, and questions you never thought you'd have to ask.

This book was born out of those kinds of stories. They are not stories with tidy endings or easy answers, but stories of women who have walked through the unraveling and found something sacred on the other side. Stories of grief and grace, of letting go and starting over. Stories of rediscovering not just what was lost, but who they truly are.

If you're holding this book, I want you to know this: you are not alone. Whether your divorce was unexpected or long overdue, whether you were left or had to leave, whether you feel mostly relief or mostly heartache, you are seen. And you are still deeply loved by a God who hasn't left your side for a moment.

Each chapter in this collection offers something a little different: truth-telling, gentle encouragement, practical wisdom, and hard-earned hope. Some of these women are just a few steps ahead of you; others have walked this road for years. But all of them understand the ache, and the possibility, of life after divorce.

My prayer is that as you read, you'll breathe a little deeper. I hope shame will lose its grip and you'll begin to believe you don't have to have it all figured out to be walking toward healing. I pray you can see that, even here, even now, you are still becoming the woman God made you to be.

This is not the end of your story.

It's a new beginning. And you don't have to walk it alone.

About the Chapters

*B*ridget Gengler opens the collection with a raw and honest reflection on the moment her marriage ended and the overwhelming grief that followed. In her chapter, she shares how God met her in the middle of her despair and gently began to lead her toward healing. Her story is a powerful reminder that we can still take steps forward even when we can't see the road ahead.

In chapter two, Julie Smith takes readers deep into the emotional wreckage of betrayal. With courageous vulnerability, she shares how she learned to move through devastation with God's help, ultimately finding strength, resilience, and joy on the other side. Her chapter is an invitation to believe that healing is possible, even when our hearts feel shattered.

In *Weathering the Storm, Welcoming the Sun*, Jennifer Burchill shares her journey of moving from uprooted to rising strong. Through practical insight and spiritual truth, she encourages women to anchor themselves in God's promises as they rebuild after the storm of divorce, learning to plant new roots and welcome new seasons.

Takhia Gaither offers practical and faith-centered guidance in her chapter filled with gentle wisdom on self-care during the chaos of divorce. She reminds readers that pouring from an empty cup is not sustainable, and that tending to your spiritual, emotional, and physical well-being is not selfish, but sacred.

Amy L. Boyd draws from Psalm 31 in chapter five, walking readers through the deeply spiritual process of lament. She demonstrates how God meets us in our tears, honors our grief, and invites us into healing through honest, vulnerable relationship with Him.

In *Hope in Every Season*, Angela King Bley shares her personal story of discovering God's faithfulness through each season after her divorce. Her chapter is filled with grace and gentle encouragement, showing how even winter seasons can be sacred spaces where hope begins to bloom.

Amber Brandt writes with authenticity and tenderness in chapter seven. She reflects on how verbal abuse and rejection nearly erased her sense of self, but through time, counseling, and the love of God, she began to rediscover her worth. Her chapter affirms that you don't need to return to "Plan A" when God's new plan is one of beauty and restoration.

Ashley Boswell shines a light on the destructive effects of gaslighting in her chapter. Drawing from her work as a counselor and her own experience, she equips readers with truth from Scripture to break free from manipulation and reclaim their God-given identity.

In chapter ten, Stephanie Lauren Jordan shares her story of brokenness and restoration after a short-lived marriage and devastating divorce during the early days of the pandemic. With hope and clarity, she describes how she moved from heartbreak to healing by embracing a new life led by God's purpose.

About the Chapters

Terra Richards closes the book with *Trust Fall: Trusting God That I Am Not Alone*. In her deeply personal chapter, she writes about the fear of being alone after a 25-year marriage ended. Through humor, faith, and vulnerability, she reminds us that even when life falls apart, God never lets us fall too far.

Chapter 1

Trusting the Journey Through the Unknown

By Bridget Gengler

"FOR WE WALK BY FAITH, NOT BY SIGHT."
2 CORINTHIANS 5:7 (ESV)

The bright sun had just dipped below the horizon, and darkness began to fill the room like a thick, suffocating blanket engulfing everything in its path. A heavy silence settled in the room as if time itself had paused. I reached for something to hold on to, my fingers brushing the rug's soft, worn, colorful fibers beneath me. It had always been there, but now, in this stillness, it felt different—more familiar, like an unexpected comfort in a place I least expected. Yet, the moment I allowed myself to breathe, the tears began falling. Each teardrop was the silent echo of the reality I could no longer escape.

That night, I collapsed in the center of my living room floor, overwhelmed by an ocean of sorrow. Tears streamed down my face—tears of sadness, loss, brokenness, and uncertainty. They fell incessantly, like rain in a violent storm, each drop reflecting the weight pressing against my chest. My body trembled with the reality of it all, the memory of his words—the moment he told me he wanted a divorce—replaying over and over in my mind. My body shook with despair as if the air around me had thickened in grief. At that moment, I truly believed that my pain would swallow me up and suffocate everything I once knew about hope.

I was consumed by hopelessness, lost in a thick darkness, and couldn't see a single step ahead. Sitting on the floor, I wept in agony that seemed to overwhelm every part of me. My body trembled with the weight of the pain, each sob coming from the deepest corners of my soul. Every inch of my body ached, and it felt as though life itself had abandoned me. I was alone, trapped in emptiness, with a hurt so overpowering that I couldn't comprehend its depths. I had never known a sorrow so deep and a grief so profound. My desperate cries pierced the silent air as if they did not come from my lips but from the very essence of my being.

A few months later, on an evening when my children were with their father, I found myself alone again, trapped in that same pit of hopelessness. The sadness weighed heavily on my heart, but eventually, my hunger nudged me out of the darkness, and I decided to grab a bite to eat.

I drove into the familiar drive-thru lane, the car moving slowly as I waited for someone to take my order. The quietness of the evening and my thoughts took me away for a moment, but then, as I sat waiting, I began to hear a conversation drift from the tables outside the restaurant. A man's voice reached me first, and something in it mirrored my feelings—hollow, desperate, lost. He was speaking to a woman, sharing the raw truth of his life, describing how drugs had taken over and how he felt trapped in a never-ending cycle with no escape in sight.

Then the woman's voice came through, so gentle but firm. She spoke of hope in a way I had never heard before.

She said, "You are never alone. God sees you, He loves you, and He wants to save you. Even in your darkest moment, there is light, and you can find a friend in God."

She spoke of God's love—how there was hope even in his brokenness. No matter how far gone he felt, God would never abandon him.

I leaned forward in my seat, the weight of her words penetrating deep into my whole body. But then, just as the conversation fell into a brief silence, something unexpected happened. The woman stood up, and I saw her, for the first time, through the slight gap between the drive-thru menu sign and my car. She locked eyes with me, and in that instant, it felt as if the world had paused. Without saying a word, she nodded, a silent affirmation, as if to say, *God is here for you, too.* Her eyes were kind, and that brief moment, that small gesture, shattered the silence in my soul. In that fleeting exchange, I somehow knew I was not as alone as I had felt.

A brief encounter with a woman at the drive-thru was the most powerful time for me in this season of life. It was an answer to my prayers. God was using this young woman to share His faithfulness and His greatness. That was the moment when I felt there was hope. I felt like I was still loved, valued, and essential.

I was meant to be in that drive-thru lane at that exact moment that evening to hear that message.

From then on, I began to understand that there was hope in the hard. Even though I was living a real-life nightmare and feeling completely broken and overwhelmed by disappointment, that tiny gesture reminded me that even when I couldn't see the path ahead, God would be faithful to heal and restore my brokenness and disappointments.

My cries to Jesus on my living room floor led to this moment. God hears us in our brokenness and allows us to be in the right place at the right time.

It was the turning point when I began to walk by faith, even if I did not know what the future would hold for my children and me. It was the instant I started to hold onto the scripture in 2 Corinthians 5:7, where Paul tells us to *walk by faith and not by sight.*

Brokenness Opens the Door to Healing, Hope, and Help from God and Others

When divorce darkens our path and leaves us uncertain, we must find a way to guide us toward the light and the road that will lead us to a brighter future.

Divorce can take every part of our souls and break them into pieces, leaving us broken like a butterfly with an injured wing. In divorce, our hearts are broken, our dreams shattered. Our souls may become lost and fall into a deep hole we wish to crawl out of, but don't know how to escape. It makes us feel like our lives are over and no future is in sight. The disappointment, heartache, and brokenness are so deep. They leave us with unbearable pain that penetrates our bodies.

Even in the depths of this pain, God remains. He is by our side every step of the way. He has not left us in these darkest moments of our lives. But He does ask us to trust—trust in the unknown. Even though we do not know what the future holds, He's carrying us. He hears us, and He listens to what we need.

Trust in Him. Begin by talking to Him; sit in prayer and share your suffering with Him. Let Him know how you are feeling. Believe that He will lead you from the depths of your despair and into a renewed future full of hope.

During this season, I learned to trust in God when:

- I sat alone in fear.
- When the road was so broken that I could no longer walk.
- When I cried out to Him in the depths of my pain.
- When I was unsure if I could pay the next bill.
- When I had to mow the lawn for the first time.
- When I became a single mom and realized that I had to do it all on my own.
- When I had to wake up with a smile on my face for my babies, when all I wanted to do was crawl back into bed.

Through all these times of uncertainty, hardship, and firsts, I found that the only way to trudge through was to surrender my struggles to God. I realized He would never leave me or forsake me, and I could trust him with these seemingly impossible realities I felt like I was facing alone.

Often, it's easy to feel like we have to walk the path alone, but we do not have to. We frequently underestimate the power of seeking support. When we are faced with profound emotional challenges, like the pain of divorce, it is easy to feel lost in our brokenness and uncertainty, even when we're relying on God and his guidance. We must find someone we trust—a friend, support group, or therapist—who will listen without judgment and help us gain a new perspective on our situation.

Working with a therapist was another turning point for me. It wasn't just about finding someone to talk to, but also about finding someone who helped me understand that my happiness does not come from someone else but rather from myself. She was able to help me reframe my thinking— *Someone does not make me happy, but rather, I am happy with someone else.* Too often, we place the responsibility for our joy on others, but the actual healing comes when we recognize that we must love ourselves first.

With this healing, we gain clarity into what we were unable to see when we were married. In my marriage, I found myself setting my dreams and desires aside for the sake of my spouse, and I began to live for his dreams and desires. We may become so entwined with another person that we lose sight of ourselves, neglecting our own needs and goals in the process. It is easy to forget that we must nurture and heal our inner selves.

Through prayer and support from others, clarity begins to appear. A clearer picture of who we are surfaces, and through brokenness comes the ability to create a better version of ourselves. When life feels like it is falling apart, we may feel lost and unseen, but through help and reflection, a better perspective of who we are and who we are meant to be starts to emerge.

You do not have to face it alone. Take time to reflect on your growth by rebuilding yourself. Taking care of yourself will better equip you to offer your best to others, especially your children, and find the strength to create the life you want.

During this time, I learned the importance of and made it a point to set aside "me" time. For me, this looked like ...

- Journaling my feelings
- Sitting down in prayer
- Writing in a gratitude journal
- Calling a friend
- Getting coffee with a friend
- Taking a walk
- Reading a book

Some other ways you might set aside time for yourself could be:

- Block the time off on your calendar.
- Wake up 15-20 minutes earlier for some quiet time.
- Take yourself on a mini date to the coffee shop, a manicure, or a walk in the park.

This time committed to self-care and healing gives us the clarity we need to understand who we are and what we need.

Once these things become clearer, it gives us the ability to see hope again. Amid a painful divorce, hope can become the lifeline that carries us through those difficult moments. Hope isn't just wishing for a better future, but believing that things will improve, even if we cannot see it now. For me, hope was the belief that even though my children would grow up in two homes, they would still experience the love of both parents and extended family. Hope is trusting that God's plan for us is bigger than anything we could have imagined, even in the hardest of times.

Hope is the steady hand reaching out to guide us through the darkness. It can sustain us through pain, sadness, and disappointment. No matter how heavy our pain is, we still have hope to guide us. It can give you strength and belief that better days are ahead.

Walking by faith, not by sight, creates a path of hope that leads us to new beginnings, where we gain clarity and develop a love for ourselves, which enables us to create the best version of ourselves.

Five ways to walk by faith, not by sight

1. Pray first, not last. Tell God what you need and maintain a constant conversation with Him.
2. Trust in the unknown and remain open to God's work in your life.
3. Keep moving forward even when you don't know what lies ahead. Life may be unsure, but keep taking small steps toward the unknown.
4. Surround yourself with believers—people who choose faith over fear.

5. Remember all the blessings from the past—write them down in a journal to remind you of the goodness in your life.

Joy in the Midst: Holding onto Hope and Faith Through Disappointment

While going through a divorce, it may seem impossible to find hope. Divorce is a painful experience that leaves us wrestling with our emotions and never-ending thoughts that may lead us in several different directions. It is easy to feel lost and discouraged when we lose the dreams we once had.

Though it may feel like our world has just been shattered, it can become an opportunity for transformation. We can rebuild, redefine, and rise from uncertainty to become the best version of ourselves. Sometimes, pain is the catalyst for personal growth and the rediscovery of our true selves.

In discovering our true selves, we realize that our dreams are evolving, not lost or shattered. It can feel like our dreams are destroyed when we go through divorce—dreams of life plans, dreams for the family, dreams of the future, and dreams for our children—and are replaced with disappointments.

The truth is, our dreams are not lost forever. They might change or evolve, but we can dream again with more clarity and wisdom. Our dreams may no longer look the same, but they are still worth pursuing and can be even greater than we had imagined.

Allowing yourself to dream again is an integral part of the healing process. There will be moments of struggle and doubt, but each day brings you closer to your worth and power to shape your new future. Divorce does not define you, and it is not your identity. It is a chapter filled with suffering and challenges, preparing you for a new and exciting chapter and the rest of your story.

If nothing else, hold onto this: **Your future is still full of possibility**, and you are worthy of the love, joy, and peace ahead of you. Hope, healing, and new dreams are just up ahead, waiting for you.

Through the disappointments in divorce, many unexpected outcomes can occur.

Truths to Carry You through the Storm

1. Seek Joy

The disappointment of divorce can make you feel like joy is out of reach. The miracle, though, is this: Joy is all around you. You just have to find it.

For me, joy came in those moments I spent with my children. Despite my brokenness and disappointments, my precious children were my blessing. I began to look at the world around me through their eyes.

The wonder of a new day.

The excitement in a hug.

The sweet kisses from their little lips.

The beauty of their laughter.

The smiles in their eyes.

The enthusiasm in my son's "happy feet".

The preciousness of my daughter's little voice.

These moments made me realize I didn't have time to sit in my disappointments and wallow in self-pity. I learned to cherish the small joys that each day brings.

Where can you find joy amid your hurt and disappointments? If you look closely, small moments can bring you joy.

The laughter in the air.

The smile of a stranger.

The flowers on the table.

The text from a friend.

The phone call from a family member.

There is beauty and joy even in the smallest things.

2. Cling to Hope

In this journey through divorce and self-discovery, what kept me afloat and moving forward was the hope that the days would get better and that God's plans for me were much bigger than I had anticipated.

I was reminded of God's promise in Jeremiah: "'For I know the plans I have for you,' says the Lord. 'They are plans for good and not for disaster, to give you a future and a hope.'" (Jeremiah 29:11, NLT). This reminder made me realize God had much more in store for my life.

What if you believed the same?

God has plans for you. Whatever you may be feeling at this moment and whatever sadness or hurt exists, what if you trust in the Lord and believe that His plans are much greater than you could ever imagine?

Ways to Trust God in the Unknown and cling to hope
- Read scripture every day.
- Write down scripture verses that remind you of His faithfulness.
- Keep those verses visible and post them somewhere so you can be reminded of them.
- Begin every day in prayer, even when you may not feel like it.
- Live in gratitude. Thank God daily, even for the little things. That gratitude can train your heart to trust Him.

3. Practice Gratitude

How could I not be grateful for everything I went through if I had faith that God would take it all and do something good with it? Paul reminds us of this promise in Philippians 1 when he says: "*And I am sure of this, that he who began a good work in you will bring it to completion at the day of Jesus Christ.*" (Philippians 1:6, ESV)

I genuinely believe in this promise. God takes our times of struggle, disappointment, pain, and shame and creates within us something that will serve the world. Even today, I know that the work is incomplete—those moments of disappointment continue to build the good work in me and help me grow. Instead of viewing myself as a victim, I constantly remind myself that there is something much better to come if I believe and trust that God is working for me.

This promise is also true for you.

Disappointments, brokenness, and suffering do not define you. They are not a predictor of your future or a definition of your past. They are part of your story. This suffering from divorce does not dictate your life or your future.

I encourage you to take time to practice gratitude. Here are some ways to implement it into your everyday life:

- Begin a gratitude journal and every day write down three things that you are grateful for. Add an affirmation at the end to remind yourself that you are enough.
- Start and end your day with thanks.
- Write a note or letter to someone and tell them what they mean to you.
- Notice small things.
- Mindful walking: As you take a walk, focus on your surroundings and name things for which you are grateful.

4. Lean on God

Divorce creates the lowest of lows. Brokenness and disappointment can engulf our souls and bury us in a deep hole of murky water. It can leave us with a sadness that feels impossible to escape. All the expectations, hopes, and dreams we envision for our future disappear.

But the strength God provides when you put your trust in Him can be life-saving, helping you keep navigating the unknown path ahead.

Stop and yield to the Lord when you feel severe disappointments and don't think you have the strength to endure it all. He is there to support you, carry you, and walk beside you when you feel like you can't go a step further. Trust in Him, and He will bring peace in those times of brokenness and sadness.

Talk to him. He hears you. . Pray and share your sadness, disappointments, worries, and fears with him. He is ready to listen.

Even in your darkest moments of divorce, God has never left you. He is right beside you, leading you through the unknown into a beautiful new future. Trust in Him and rely on His strength when you feel weak. This time is temporary. There will be new smiles, adventures, laughter, and opportunities. Just continue to hold onto the hope that those days are yet to come.

Closing Prayer for Guidance and Peace

As we end this time together, I would like to offer a prayer that helped guide me through the most challenging days of my divorce.

Dear Heavenly Father,

In this season of change, I turn to You for guidance and peace. As I walk through the storm of divorce, help me to remember I am not alone. Even when the path is unclear, teach me to walk by faith, not by sight.

Give me the strength to trust in Your plan, knowing that You are with me in every step of this transition. Help me lean on others when needed and bring people to me who will walk alongside me. Fill my heart with Your peace that surpasses all understanding, and guide me toward healing and growth through this season.

Though the path may be dark, lead me to the light, where I may find hope in Your promises and renew my faith, knowing that You are leading me toward a future full of grace and transformation.

I trust You, Lord, with my pain, uncertainty, and heart.

In Jesus' name, I pray.

Amen

Next Steps

As you navigate this season of divorce, here are some suggestions for next steps that may guide you as you face an uncertain future and rediscover yourself.

1. Create a quiet time during the day to pray, journal, and express gratitude.
2. Seek support from a therapist, church community, or trusted individual.
3. Find joy in your day.
4. Focus on the blessings, however big or small.
5. Give yourself permission to invest in "me time" and find clarity in who God created you to be.

Chapter 2

Betrayal and Brokenness: Thriving Through the Pain

By Julie Smith

"BUT TWO CHOICES ON THE SHELF: PLEASING GOD OR PLEASING SELF." COMMONLY ATTRIBUTED TO KEN COLLIER[1]

I came home from the doctor's office after a post-op visit. When I opened the door and stepped in, I immediately felt a heaviness in the air. Something wasn't right. I walked through the living room into the dining room, and there it was. The family picture was gone. He was gone. My heart shattered into a million pieces.

This wasn't the first time he had left, nor would it be the last. His choices affected the whole family. The children's hearts would be broken again, and that was what hurt the most. How would we survive?

I knew things weren't great between us. There were red flags from the beginning that grew over the years, which I chose to ignore. I thought my love and faith would keep us together. I was wrong.

---

[1] Quote attributed to Ken Collier; original source unverified.

I had a hysterectomy a couple of weeks before he left. He had gotten mean and hateful towards me to the point of verbal abuse. He called me names that were demeaning. He made me feel as if I couldn't do anything right. One night, I was sitting on the couch. He went to the refrigerator and stood there saying, "I hate you! Do you know how much I despise you? " The attack was unprovoked. I was shocked and deeply hurt.

It was an abusive relationship. He hit me on several occasions, which left bruises. I lied about what caused them, especially my black eye. That was hard to miss. He was a narcissist who belittled and made fun of me. Life was like walking on eggshells, especially if he had been drinking.

He left without saying anything. He just didn't come home from work. My husband took all the money out of our checking account, and the car that ran. He called later that night to tell me where he was and that he wasn't coming home. I begged him to come home for the sake of the children. He refused.

He became involved in another affair, which sent thoughts swirling through my head. Why wasn't I enough for him? What could I have done differently to make him want to stay? Why doesn't he love me anymore? What can I do to get him to want to come home?

I was deeply wounded and alone. I had four children to raise by myself. They were 2, 4, 6, and 8. I fought through my own pain and put my arms around my precious children and held them close as we grieved our loss. They didn't understand. Especially the two youngest. It broke my heart every time they asked when Daddy was coming home.

How do you leave your children? Drugs. Alcohol. Women. Selfishness. His decisions caused us nothing but pain.

Going to church was difficult because I was no longer part of a couple. But I wasn't single either. Friends and family were supportive, but after the fellowship was over, I still went home alone with four young children. It was hard taking care of them 24/7 without any help. I longed for companionship, and I didn't have close female friends to spend time with. I wasn't invited to parties that involved couples. I felt isolated. I was mad at my husband for putting me in a situation I did not want to be in, and mad at God because He could have stopped him from leaving. No hope was in sight. I envisioned all the years ahead of me being alone. Depression set in, and I wondered, "How can I keep going?

Going through a divorce or separation is never easy, no matter the circumstances. Fear of the unknown is frequently at the forefront of your mind. You don't know what the future holds. These are legitimate concerns that need to be faced. There's a change in your finances, custody battles, and strained extended family relationships. You may be displaced from your home. Where are you going to live? Can I even afford to move? Who's going to keep the children while I work to support us? Where will I be able to find a job? Life as you knew it is gone. Now it's a mess.

How do you proceed? Your mind is full of "what ifs," "whys," and "what nows." You feel your brain is overwhelmed. And it is. You try to move forward. You can't seem to focus on anything. You take one step ahead. Next thing you know, you're two steps behind. It goes on and on like a merry-go-round.

If infidelity is involved in the breakdown of the marriage, as in my case, other emotions flood your heart and mind. Why wasn't I enough? What did I do to cause him/her to desire someone else? You're riddled with pain and guilt. Anger inflames your soul. You feel betrayed by the one person who was supposed to love you the most for a lifetime. You want revenge. To lash out, hoping it will make you feel better and ease the pain. But it doesn't. The pain is still there. You've made an even bigger mess.

You begin to internalize your thoughts and emotions. "I'm not enough." "I can't do anything right!" "I'm not lovable." "Nobody will ever love me." Thoughts like these play on a continuous loop in your mind. Over and over. Day after day. You go through the motions of doing what has to be done, but you're not really there. You retreat into yourself. Depression moves in. You become a person nobody recognizes anymore. You're a shell of who you were.

Imagine gluing two boards together. Someone grabs them and pulls them apart. When you look at the inside of the boards, there are splinters. They didn't break evenly. Each board has a part of the other board still attached. It's not a clean break. This is what divorce/separation looks like.

Often, you blame God. You may think that's outrageous, and you'd never do such a thing. That's what I thought, too, but I did! Subtle thoughts of, "Why, God, did You let this happen to me? God, you could have stopped it if You wanted to!" Your mind takes off and feeds on blaming God. Now you feel cut off from Him, too.

All of these are perfectly normal reactions. You're hurting and don't know how or where to direct the overwhelming pain and anger. Some people keep it bottled up inside. Others let it explode whenever and wherever they can. The least little thing will set them off. They're a walking time bomb. When the explosion occurs, nothing and no one is safe. Destruction everywhere. Hot tears may accompany the explosion.

You survey the rubble. Guilt immediately rushes into your soul. You begin to pick up the pieces. You apologize and seek to repair what is broken, which includes the hearts of those who were caught up in the blast.

I went through all of these emotions. It was like being on a roller coaster. Up, down, and all around. I tried to keep it together for my children. At night, when I finally fell into bed, I was exhausted physically and emotionally. Lonely and overwhelmed. It was then that I let the tears come. Sometimes, heartrending sobs would erupt from the depths of my soul. I could no longer keep them in.

It felt like I was carrying a heavy weight, and my life as a wife was over. I mechanically went through each day focusing on what needed to be done, trying to meet the needs of my children. My heart felt heavy, yet hollow. Sorrow was my constant companion. I was weary and worn. Again, I cried out to God in anger, "Why did you let him leave? What am I supposed to do now without him?" I wearily sat down to rest after my tirade. I picked up my favorite book. It has stories full of hope. It tells me of a God who loves me.

I began meeting with a woman from church who had been through a similar situation. She pointed me back to the Bible. She also shared verses with me that encouraged me, such as, "Be strong and of a good courage, fear not, nor be afraid of them: for the LORD thy God, he it is that doth go with thee; he will not fail thee, nor forsake thee" (Deuteronomy 31:6, KJV). That reminded me that I wasn't alone. God was with me to comfort and take care of me. I began to read the Bible again.

God spoke to my heart that I needed to forgive my husband. Even though he had done some horrible things, he was worthy of forgiveness. God has forgiven me for all the bad deeds and thoughts I have had. If He could forgive me, I should forgive my husband. It wasn't easy, but I did. I asked God to forgive me for my part in the breakdown of our marriage. God filled my heart with forgiveness towards the one who betrayed me. He released the bitterness that had sprung up. You know? An amazing thing happened in my heart as I actively forgave him. I began to have compassion for him and started praying for him. It didn't change my circumstances. He didn't come running back home, but my heart was still. I could feel alive again. My heart felt light. All the anger and bitterness were gone. God filled my heart with hope.

You may be thinking about your situation. Maybe he hasn't asked for forgiveness. Perhaps he/she doesn't see anything wrong with what he/she has done, nor wants to change. My husband didn't ask for forgiveness either, but I still forgave. I did it for me so God could work in my heart. As long as I had bitterness, there was no room for love. I didn't want to carry that heavy burden.

Forgiveness is an action. A choice. Even though you have forgiven someone, it doesn't mean it doesn't come up in your mind from time to time, along with the anger.

Each time this happens, forgive them again. You could say to yourself, "I have already forgiven them and I am no longer angry." Forgiveness is rarely a one-time event.

Recovery from infidelity and divorce is not a straight line. Some say you will get over it in time, or they say don't let this break you, ... there is a lot of advice. The fact is, this is something you will carry for the rest of your life, like a person who recovers from a severe injury or illness. It will always be a part of you. But you don't have to let it limit you, own you, or define you. You can pick up the pieces and build a good new life from them. Your family and your faith can be the tools that allow you to do that. You will always have the scar, but in time, it can be a badge of honor showing you survived, you prevailed. With that can come a sense of value and self-worth you may have lost, or never had.

When you have thoughts of unworthiness stemming from your past, look yourself in the mirror and focus on what God says you are. You are loved. "I have loved thee with an everlasting love" (Jeremiah 31:3, KJV). God's love for you will never change. He loved you before you were born, He loves you now and will continue to love you through all eternity. It's not dependent on anything you do or don't do. His love for you will never end.

You are unique. "I am fearfully and wonderfully made" (Psalm 139:14, KJV). You are chosen. "I have chosen you" (John 15:16b, KJV). For years, you have endured negative programming, which is now wired into your mind. It will take time and work to overcome the negative by focusing on the truth. God created you as one of a kind. When He was creating you, I believe God smiled and said, "Look at her/

him. She/he is perfect." You have been chosen for greatness. God has a special plan for your life that only you can do. He has given you gifts and talents that people around you need. Look around you. Let God's love flow through you. God is smiling down on you, just as you are!

"And be not conformed to this world: but be ye transformed by the renewing of your mind, that ye may prove what is that good, and acceptable, and perfect, will of God" (Romans 12:2,KJV). Look for verses that apply to your situation. When these negative thoughts come to you, counteract them with scripture. For example, your thoughts are telling you, "You're not good enough. Nobody will ever love me." Remember the verses above? God loves you and has chosen you. Friends and family love you. Don't let the negative thoughts win! Ask God for help. Find a friend or mentor to help you and support you. Over time, you will start believing what God says and forgetting the lies you heard for so long.

At the beginning of this chapter, I mentioned that this was not the first time or the last time he left. A couple of years later, I was at home one day. My husband walked into my house without warning. He said he wanted to come back. I told him if he was serious, he needed to talk to our pastor and to my dad. If they both thought he was sincere, he could stay. He went and talked to each of them separately. My pastor and father believed he was indeed sincere. I fixed a nice supper. We ate as a complete family for the first time in several years. It was a little awkward. The children weren't sure how to act with their dad, but they soon warmed up to him.

The next morning, I got the oldest kids ready and took them to school. When I returned, my husband said, "I can't do this." I begged him to stay, but he chose not to. I swore then and there that I was not going to put myself or my children through this anymore. My heart was broken again, and so were my children's. Again, I chose to forgive, but this time I set up boundaries. He no longer had access to me or my children. Forgiveness doesn't mean you have to let them back into your life.

A few years later, my husband decided to file for a divorce. I didn't want it, but had no choice. I waived his paying child support if he would relinquish parental rights. He agreed. He had not had any contact with the children anyway since he left again.

Choices have consequences. He missed watching his children grow up. All the milestones. The weddings. The births of grandchildren and their accomplishments.

I don't know your specific situation, but I do know that God is with you each step of the way. He still has good plans for you and your life. "'For I know the plans I have for you,' says the Lord. 'They are plans for good and not for disaster, to give you a future and a hope'" (Jeremiah 29:11, NLT).

Look for the small everyday miracles He sends. The laughter of a child and the beauty of creation are two examples. Look around you. Pay attention as you go through your day. Perhaps you see a flower growing through the broken concrete. A symbol of yourself rising up in strength and beauty. A precious gift of God.

I wear a silver butterfly necklace to signify the transformation God has done in my own life. "Therefore if any man be in Christ, he is a new creature: old things are passed away; behold, all things are become new" (2 Corinthians 5: 17, KJV). I am not burdened and weighed down by my past. God is creating a new life for me. I am free to fly.

Your circumstances may be very different, but you are hurting. Trying to make sense of it all. You're unsure of where to turn. How to move forward. Your divorce or separation does not define your life. You can have a fresh start.

Next Steps

May I suggest writing your thoughts in a journal? Perhaps find some verses that are special to you. Look for the everyday miracles. Put them in the journal. Over time, you will see how you've grown and changed. What is terrifying to you now will, as you journal, be a testimony that you survived. From brokenness to healing. From betrayal to forgiveness. Not only survived, but you thrived.

I'll be praying for each of you as you read this book. It was written to encourage you by sharing our stories. You are not alone!

Chapter 3

Weathering the Storm, Welcoming the Sun: From Uprooted to Rooted & Rising

By Jennifer Burchill

"BUT BLESSED ARE THOSE WHO TRUST IN THE LORD AND HAVE MADE THE LORD THEIR HOPE AND CONFIDENCE. THEY ARE LIKE TREES PLANTED ALONG A RIVERBANK, WITH ROOTS THAT REACH DEEP INTO THE WATER. SUCH TREES ARE NOT BOTHERED BY THE HEAT OR WORRIED BY LONG MONTHS OF DROUGHT. THEIR LEAVES STAY GREEN, AND THEY NEVER STOP PRODUCING FRUIT."

JEREMIAH 17:7-8 (NLT)

I remember sitting in my car nervously debating whether to walk into the 50th birthday party my friend was throwing for her husband, looking around the parking lot to see if I recognized any cars. Should I turn around and retreat home to safety, feigning a headache or last-minute conflict? I felt a pit in my stomach, followed by an overwhelming sense of smallness, of solitude. I was overcome by the sudden realization that I would be attending parties like this by myself from now on. My new normal for social events was solo, without someone waiting at the table for me, to share small talk with, without someone to help escape those inevitable, uncomfortable party conversations, to laugh and leave with, to be my home base.

After a few minutes of going back and forth, tapping my fingernails on the steering wheel, I braved it and went in, knowing that stalling in the car wasn't going to make it easier; it was something I was going to have to get used to. And I'm not going to lie, it wasn't like the social events of the past, where I enjoyed catching up with couples and friends. There was an uneasiness upon entering, with a quick and desperate sweep around the room for any familiar faces. I knew the host, but she was busy hostessing. Some of the guests were acquaintances, but not friends. I recognized some who lived in my former neighborhood, where we lived as a family. A few I had seen at school functions. Most were strangers. I felt relief when I spotted one person I knew from a club I once belonged to, but that had stopped meeting a few years prior, and I hadn't seen her since. I sought her out, but instead of the normal friendly banter, I found I no longer knew how to respond to the simple, "Hey, long time no-see, how are you?" My inner dialogue was racing: "Do I not tell them and pretend everything is okay, or tell them and risk bringing the party atmosphere down?" I felt ungrounded, certainly uprooted.

I stayed at the party for as long as I could before I felt like I was starting to garner unwanted sympathy for being alone, since I had no one to really talk to or sit with. Then, I left. On my way home, I realized I had come across as a socially awkward person because I didn't know how to engage in small talk. Without somebody there at my side, I not only felt like an outsider but also suddenly self-conscious and very much uncomfortable in social situations.

This continued for a few years that followed. Company Christmas parties that I used to look forward to, I now dreaded attending as I was the odd one at a table of couples with the empty chair beside me. When you are operating from an emotional place (and boy was I ever), you aren't at your best. In retrospect, there were moments of oversharing, probably to the point of my making others uncomfortable. They didn't know what to say or how to react to the updates I was sharing with them. There were moments of not knowing how truthful or how much to divulge. There were many moments of feeling like I didn't belong now that I was no longer part of the "couples culture."

Feeling like an outsider transferred into daily areas of my life—going into school functions, band concerts, and soccer matches, having to walk in by myself, scoping out the venue, hoping I was not going to run into or accidentally sit near my ex. When I realized that this was my new norm, it was devastatingly sad to feel alone and know that social situations were not going to be the same, but tinged with anxiety. I no longer had the spouse who was the extrovert to my introvert, and I could no longer sit comfortably in the role of the observer. I experienced conversations that no longer felt relatable. I began questioning friendships and my ability to connect with people from my pre-divorce life.

I vividly remember a dinner party with friends where I was the only single person. Everyone was happily married and in an animated conversation about how much their spouses were lamenting that they didn't get to spend enough time with them. They were complaining that they didn't get any time to themselves, saying things like, "He wants to go on vacation with just me," and how they just wanted time to themselves. I couldn't relate. I both had nothing to contribute to the conversation and felt pangs of jealousy, not of them but of their partnerships. I felt less than. I wondered if I even fit in the group now. We were living different experiences, my married friends and I, and I didn't know that I belonged anymore. It was a lonely moment, sitting around a table of familiar faces who felt so far away.

My new normal post-divorce was a shock, with aftershocks continuing with each first I experienced as a newly single person. One of these aftershocks I experienced after reflecting on a parenting magazine article that discussed the effects of divorce on children. What I took away from it was how, as parents, we spend our lives trying to protect our kids, yet we're the ones inflicting this hurt on them, uprooting their stability. That realization sat with me for a long time, I felt it deeply, and it hit hard. I was discouraged, felt like a failure, and was terrified for myself and for my kids. At the same time, it allowed me to step out of my view and think about it from the kids' perspective. It made me more hyper-focused on protecting them. Although I felt a tremendous sense of guilt about it, I also knew that what I was doing, I needed to do in order to be here for them, for the future that was on the horizon.

Let Go of What No Longer Serves You

But as things settled, what was on the horizon was a slowly growing sense of hope for a better, more peaceful life for all of us. And that hope on that new horizon started when I learned to let go of what was no longer serving me.

- Letting go of guilt and accepting that change was necessary.

- Releasing the shame that I felt about not "succeeding" at marriage, instead acknowledging with appreciation that I was doing my best to protect and provide for my kids.

- Letting go of the unrealistic expectations or the vision of how I thought my life would be, what the future would look like, and embracing the unknown as exciting, and in the knowledge that God has plans for good and a future and a hope. (Jeremiah 29:11)

That notion of "not fitting in"—that was in *my* head, it wasn't coming from my friends or family. It was something I concocted and latched onto. Although they may not understand the same way that someone who had gone through a situation like mine would, they still wanted to support me. We still had a shared history, and that wasn't disappearing. So I let that go, and when I did, I was lighter.

You are not who you were pre-divorce, and you can see that as a blessing because you are resilient. You have the next chapter to look forward to, full of opportunities and unknown adventures, and experiences. I recently asked some of my divorced friends what they started feeling when they let the guilt and shame go. They shared that it provided a sense of peacefulness, of excitement around job opportunities, a sense of pride; they were proud of themselves for getting free.

I want you to experience that peacefulness too. Let go of anything that isn't serving you, whether that be guilt, shame, or your idea of how you thought your life would be. Give yourself the space to allow those roots of yours to start expanding in the soil. God gives you grace. Give yourself some.

What are some of the things you need to let go of in order to spread your roots, to grow and bloom?

Ask for the Support You Need

Even in lonely times, we do not need to wallow and stay stuck in the mud—the fastest way out is grabbing the extended helping hand that is trying to pull us out. Sometimes this means asking for what you specifically need, and doing so without feeling shame. Having our support systems is always important; they are even more crucial in the midst of or following a divorce. We know it's God's design for us to do life in community, but sometimes it's just so hard to ask for help, especially for those of us who pride ourselves on being self-reliant, or who don't want to bother others with our heavy stuff. But here's the thing—not asking may keep you stuck, feeling alone, helpless, or may even start to turn into resentment. Please don't let that happen.

Our friends and family might not know what to say to us. Those who haven't experienced divorce cannot fully understand the situation that you're in. They don't know how you're feeling, but you can't fault them for that; they haven't walked in your shoes. They most certainly want to help, but may not want to intervene, or they think we need our space. But here's the thing—they cannot read our minds on what we need and when we need it, so I encourage you to be brave and ask friends and family boldly and unapologetically. It might not be what you are used to doing, or be particularly comfortable, but I assure you that your friends and family will gather round to stand by you. You would do it for them, right? Let them do it for you.

I sure felt less lonely when I learned how to ask for support, and it might help you too. This may be something as simple as saying:

- Hey, I'm feeling lonely and would love some company. Do you want to come over?
- I would like help picking up the kids from school (or from an activity).
- Do you want to go for a walk or for coffee?
- I'm going to the football game—could you save me a seat so I don't have to sit alone?

See, that's not so scary, is it? These small acts that people likely don't even think twice about are kind and meaningful; they help us feel supported.

It's an easier ask when you have friends who have walked a similar path as you because they do know how you are feeling, and having them as our people is everything, especially during the early days. I was extremely fortunate to find a group of such women. Because I could no longer attend my former small group of couples, my pastor suggested a small group that he thought would be a good fit for me, as they were also going through or had gone through a divorce. That was several years ago, and they remain close friends. We have walked through many stages of motherhood together and through challenges: ongoing court trials, post-divorce parenting issues, but also through all sorts of life celebrations together, and we continue to do so. I couldn't have survived and thrived as well without them. Finding like-minded people to walk alongside you through your challenges, offering encouragement, a shoulder to cry on, someone to proofread your communications, and someone to laugh with—it's everything.

In what specific ways can you ask for help from someone in your community this week?

Who can you connect with who has been through a similar experience?

If no one immediately comes to mind, can you seek a small group, or women's group, or a divorce support group?

Reconnect with Joy

It's easy to lose yourself in the day-to-day of motherhood and marriage, and work. And even more so when going through a divorce. Your focus is rightly on surviving, and if you have children, making sure they come out as unscathed and supported as possible. But you also have the opportunity to reconnect with yourself, the you of your youth.

I had stopped singing because I was told early on in my marriage that I did not have an "angelic voice," but I found a renewed interest in 80s music and movies. It reminded me of a time I felt free, creative, and full of possibility. I found joy again in visiting museums, in yoga classes, in spontaneous dance parties in the kitchen while making dinner or baking with the kids. I remembered how much I loved arts and crafts, and took a pottery class.

Think about what brought you joy, what you were passionate about that may have taken a back seat. Begin exploring and diving into those things again. That may be ...

- A rediscovered joy of music or singing—new artists or new songs from old favorites
- Painting, photography, or other art
- Visiting museums and re-learning a topic you used to find interesting—we now have the Internet and don't have to pore through Encyclopedia Britannica
- Re-reading treasured novels you had forgotten about
- Browsing shops, alone, with no time limits
- Losing yourself in a bookstore or library
- Baking or cooking
- Learning a language for fun—or one you haven't studied since high school
- Writing and quiet time, reflecting
- Volunteering for a favorite cause
- Traveling to new places

What did you love to do that you lost along the way?

What joyful activities can you fill your new life with?

Freedom of Choice

There is a positive aspect to divorce I haven't heard people openly discuss, and that is the freedom divorce affords. Freedom because you can choose how you spend your time. You can choose how you spend your money. You can choose what you watch on TV (no fighting over the remote).

I missed my kids terribly when they were with their father. So instead of focusing on the piercing loneliness I felt when they weren't there, the quiet and empty-feeling house, after a while, I shifted into asking myself, "What can I do with this time that I normally can't?"

Sometimes this meant eating a bowl of cereal for dinner (no kitchen clean up!) Sometimes I would sleep on the couch, curled up with the dog, and not even go up to bed (no bed to make!) Regular dinners with my small group were part of a new routine. The freedom of choice was easy to embrace.

Another flavor of freedom came from the understanding that I didn't have to accept every invitation, and you, too, can choose personal happiness over social expectations. This is your time, don't waste it by feeling obligated to go anywhere or do anything you don't want to. You need to nourish yourself to flourish, and it's ok to say no or to alter traditions and celebrations to reflect what is personally meaningful to you.

My parents wanted to throw me a party for my 50th birthday. I was used to being invited to and seeing milestone birthday celebrations thrown by people's spouses. Although it was a sweet offer that I appreciated and was touched by, I was uncomfortable with this idea. But after pondering it, I realized I didn't have to do something traditional. I decided this was my 50th birthday, and I was going to celebrate it, but I would celebrate it in a way that was meaningful to me. That meant not a big party at a local restaurant or bar, or someone's home, but surrounded by what made me feel supported throughout and following the divorce.

Going to yoga was a respite for me because when I was there, I wasn't worried about parenting issues, lawyer bills, or feeling the unnecessary stress that comes from high-conflict divorce. This was the one place where I could be in the moment and breathe and enjoy. So, for my 50th birthday party, I rented the yoga studio and invited my friends and family members who would enjoy it (not something my brothers or dad were into) to participate in a private yoga class with me. I shared words of gratitude with all who joined me. My favorite instructor led us through a reflection, and we had class followed by birthday treats in the lobby. It was the perfect way for me to celebrate moving into a new decade.

You don't have to skip out on celebrations, even if they look different now—this is your chance to reinvent your traditions in ways that are inspiring and feel true to who you are becoming. Choose what feels natural, joyful, and supportive to you, even if it doesn't follow the norm—this new chapter is yours to define, embrace, and enjoy.

There's a quiet power in realizing that even after the heartbreak, the messiness, and the moments that felt like rock bottom, you still get to choose. That's what freedom looks like—doing something beautiful with circumstances you didn't ask for.

What are some new things you can do with your time, and environment, or new routines you would like to try?

What are some upcoming celebrations you can redefine so they feel like they represent the new you?

Empowered Through Self-Sufficiency & Resilience

Another aspect of my being freshly single, one of the more practical sides, was that I no longer had a spouse with whom to navigate life's logistics. Household tasks all fell on me, and that was an overwhelming responsibility: housework, paying bills, arranging kids' activities, mowing the yard, snow shoveling, and fixing fuses going out. Something my married friends took for granted, and something I had taken for granted.

You are used to calling for your husband to replace the bulb when a light goes out, or dealing with a clogged toilet, or disposing of dead mice or birds in the yard. This was a challenge for me. My son had new responsibilities in helping, and I remember once saying, "You're the man of the house now." His young tween self swiftly replied, "I didn't ask to be." That took my breath away, and in that moment, I was struck by the fact that through no fault of their own, my kids were being asked to step up. That's when I decided that I was going to have to step up too, learn what I could, and ease their already burdened life situation. I went to the hardware store, bought a shovel, and buried the bird.

While I would never claim to be even semi-competent in the home repair arena, I have learned not to panic and accept it. Google has become a constant companion during these projects, and with each chirping battery in the smoke alarm I changed and plumbing issue I investigated, my sense of independence slowly began to climb. I watched and asked questions of the plumber. I asked the sprinkler maintenance man to show me how to turn off all of the water spigots. I asked the electrician to show me which fuse was which. A can-do attitude begins to emerge, and you learn that YouTube is a fantastic reference when searching "my disposal is not working." Embrace the confidence and self-reliance that grows when you face these challenges. Each one is an exercise that strengthens your resilience. Be proud of every "I *figured it out*" you whisper to yourself. You're more capable than you know.

What projects have you completed that allowed you to flex your resiliency?

What is something that you've done by yourself or new skills you have mastered that you wouldn't have done before that you're extremely proud of?

Becoming a Source of Support for Others

"Therefore, encourage one another and build each other up as you are already doing." 1 Thessalonians 5:11 (CSB)

I know that the lessons I've learned through this journey aren't just for me, but something I can now offer to others who are walking a similar path. When I was in the midst of the divorce, I never could have imagined the eventual day when I was on the other side of it, nor that the turmoil would subside, and that a new sense of normal would feel not only comfortable but grounded in hope and peace.

Recently, I was able to pay it forward by helping a friend by sharing some referrals and resources, and another by showing up as a willing listener with an open heart, and another by listening and conveying some of my experiences. The role of community in healing goes both ways—in my small group, we help each other through the different stages and challenges in life. Every moment of growth becomes a gift when you use it to support someone who's just beginning their own healing.

In reflecting on your growth, with gratitude, think about ways you can share your wisdom and strength to support others. You learned from others through similar lived experiences; others will learn from you. There's something powerful about turning pain into purpose—when we share our story, we remind others they're not alone.

How can you encourage and love others who may be going through similar challenges?

In what ways can your story inspire hope for someone else starting to find their way?

Time to Bloom

Now is the time to bloom into a brand new chapter of your life. You are going from rootless to rooted, and it's time to rise, your face toward the sun. Bloom into something new, something beautiful, something strong and full of resilience. Like a flower, each petal reflects your growth, your healing, your rediscovery. May this illustration be a reminder as you move forward and continue to bloom, rooted and rising!

Let go of what doesn't serve you. Release the guilt, the shame, the unrealistic expectations. Experience the peace, and delight in the space that allows you to grow in new directions.

Ask for what you need. Your people will gladly show up for you when you let them.

Reconnect with a part of yourself that has felt lost. Let joy and curiosity lead you toward a renewed sense of self. What part of yourself did you tuck away? Invite it back and let it bloom again.

Choose how you spend your time and energy. You get to choose how you show up, what you let go of, and where you pour your energy. Choose to seek joy, to lean on faith, and to rebuild a life that reflects who you are now.

Be **empowered** through self-sufficiency. Think of something you've done by yourself—something you never thought you could do. That is your proof and confidence builder.

Support and encourage others. Reach out, invite someone in, sit with them, listen, love. When you offer your support, you reinforce your own strength too.

You have walked through uncertainty, and still, you are here. There may be days when loneliness creeps in, but remember: you are never alone. Community can be expanded. Joy can be rediscovered. You are poised to create a life that fits who you are now, in this moment. May you write this next chapter in your own handwriting, full of flair and flourish—with courage, with curiosity, with compassion. You are blooming. And my friend, this is just the beginning...

Chapter 4

While Riding Through the Storm: Ways to Practice Self-Care During Divorce

By Takhia Gaither

"BUT THOSE WHO TRUST IN THE LORD WILL FIND NEW STRENGTH. THEY WILL SOAR HIGH ON WINGS LIKE EAGLES. THEY WILL RUN AND NOT GROW WEARY. THEY WILL WALK AND NOT FAINT." ISAIAH 40:31 (NLT)

I would venture to say that most people do not get married and plan to divorce. I know some people go into it saying, "Well, if it doesn't work, then I'll get one," but in general, most of us are looking for our special version of happily ever after. For the most part, you know every day won't be rainbows and butterflies, but you're expecting that more times than not, there will be. Then one day, all the "No Year Problems" start to happen. "No Year Problems" are those that should never happen during any year of marriage for any reason, especially at ongoing or consistent rates, such as infidelity, constant bickering and arguing, etc.

Sadly, I found myself attempting to deal with a series of "No Year Problems" very early in my marriage, which ultimately led to separation and divorce. The few people that I confided in when I first began the process all had the same question: "How are you feeling?" A lot of times, I didn't have an answer for them other than the obligatory "fine" because I hadn't taken the time to really think about how I felt or thought.

For years, I was a high-functioning depressive. High-functioning depressives don't actually look like the image we usually associate with those who suffer from depression. I worked every day, completed one degree program, started another, and generally lived life in what was perceived to be "normal." However, out of the public eye, everything internally was falling apart. I was always unsettled. Despite things in life seeming to be fine, I was generally unhappy. Instead of dealing with the unhappiness or trying to figure out the source of it, I would look for a new thing to do—a new degree, a new part-time job, a new hobby—anything so that I didn't have to face the unhappiness. I was raised in church, so I never wanted to accept that I was depressed.

When I finally went to God in prayer and was honest with Him and myself about what was going on, He walked me through healing. I couldn't find a therapist, the constraints of my marriage didn't even allow me the time if I had, so it was me and Jesus working it out. I didn't find out the proper name for what I was experiencing or what triggered it until a few years before my divorce, when I began seeing a counselor for recovery after domestic abuse. In times of extreme stress, I turn to things that generally make me happy, which is a good strategy, but I go too far. I look for things that will absorb every minute I have so that at the end of the day, I just sleep from exhaustion, not from rest. The next day, the cycle restarts. I had to learn the difference between wanting to do things or engage in new programs or activities because of interest, or if I was using them as a mask for depression. I prayed for my discernment to increase so that I could hear the Lord telling me whether to move or not on activities.

The difference ended up being the feeling of peace that comes with God's ideas versus the anxiety that came with mine. For example, not long after I was married, I decided to get an Associate's Degree in teacher education. Usually, people get an Associate's and then a Bachelor's, so it was confusing to some why it seemed like I was going backward. I needed to take courses to renew my teaching license, and I'd never had a formal degree in education, so it served multiple purposes. The classes were free, so it seemed like a great idea. When I finished the program in August 2020, I didn't have a plan to return to school for anything. However, when things started going bad in my marriage, I thought it would be a good idea to complete the doctoral program I started in 2007, but stopped in 2013 because I realized I started it as a way to run from depression. When I became incredibly unhappy, I spent 3 months trying to get in contact with the university to attempt to re-enroll in the doctoral program. Did I mention this was when places still weren't fully open due to the pandemic?? I was persistent in finding out a bunch of nothing, but it kept me occupied and busy, so I didn't have to deal with the unhappiness of marriage.

By the time I'd filed for divorce, I realized that I'd reached a level of perfection when it came to deflecting. I felt the wheels of anxiety turning to find another outlet, but through lots of prayer and coffee chats with Jesus, I was able to institute a few things for self-care as I was riding through the storm. In this situation, you have to be able to function and make decisions. I was trying to think of another way to say it that doesn't seem so bossy, but I can't. It's definitely a "have to." It's not optional. For me, it seemed like things were always on extremes, either nothing was happening regarding the case or everything was happening all at the same time, but you never knew which one was going to take place, so I was just as they say, "sitting on ready." Finding ways to take care of yourself and pay attention to yourself during this time is imperative. Here are a few things to try, and while you're at it, YouTube Yolanda Adams' Riding Through the Storm, it will definitely bless you. You're welcome in advance.

1. Take time for yourself. I can hear you thinking or saying out loud, "What time?" One of the things I had to implement with my children was quiet hours. I picked a specific time in the evening/night when I was off limits unless there were emergency situations. I used the time to read, pray, study, watch something I wanted to see, or sometimes, I literally did nothing! I've been divorced for three years, and this is still my #1. Everything shuts down at the same time every night, even on the weekends. You need this time to check in with yourself. It won't seem like they're complying right away, but keep at it. They will fall in with the new schedule. That leads us right into #2.

2. Don't deny what you feel. Growing up, Wonder Woman was my favorite character. She still is. I thought it was amazing that no matter how she felt, she could spring into action and get it done. I would put on my cape and deny every feeling I had about everything. I choose not to acknowledge them. I would dive into whatever task I had and keep pushing. I'm pretty sure that doing that is the fast track to an emotional or mental breakdown. At one time, I was really close to one. Part of dealing with depression was accepting that I don't and didn't have to be Wonder Woman. I was allowed to not be ok. Even if I couldn't put my feelings into words, I made it a point to recognize and admit that I was not ok. I began to write them out in journals. After I admitted it, I took it to God in prayer and gave it to Him. Sometimes, I would journal out the prayers and leave space for praise reports because I would go back, read them later, and write about the things that happened since that prayer. It gave me something to reflect on as I was rebuilding my history and relationship with God. During the "situationship" of the dating phase and the marriage, I remember feeling far away from God. Rereading the prayer and journal entries reminded me, He's always here with me.

3. Get rest. You will want to feel like you have to do EVERYTHING, ALL THE TIME. **You don't**. I put it in bold because I wanted you to know that you really don't have to! If denying feelings was the first thing on the road to mental breakdown checklist, then not getting rest has to be the second. The depression

started when I was in college. I didn't have to study in high school and had phenomenal grades. Getting poor grades in college was new for me, and I created a really random sleep and study schedule. Add that to packing on the activities, which led to just staying up and living off cat naps. During the relationship and early in the marriage, I would go so much that I had days when I would collapse. In 2009, I was diagnosed with an autoimmune condition that requires me to get proper rest. If I don't, I can end up in the ER for multiple reasons. Going back to #1, the quiet time came about because I needed time to unwind before I went to bed so that I could rest and not just kind of sleep. One thing that was extremely helpful but seems so out of pocket? Taking a nap! Even if it was just ten or fifteen minutes of my lunch break, I would set a timer and make myself lie down to do nothing. Whenever I began to feel extreme overwhelm, I would find time to take a nap. It's an automatic reset button. It also reenergizes your brain so you're not so cloudy.

4. Work with a counselor or a coach. My marriage was abusive. About two years before the divorce, I started working with a counselor as part of the services offered to the victims of domestic incidents. During the pandemic, that office closed down, and I stopped counseling for almost two years. Right before filing for the divorce, there was a second near incident, and because the police were called, they offered free counseling through the domestic violence program, which I gladly accepted! I also worked with a Christian

trauma-informed narcissistic abuse coach. The combination was phenomenal! The therapist was able to explain and help me put language to what was going on and to develop healthier strategies to deal with life and all its things. Through working with the coach, I gained insight from someone who'd gone through my present situation. Through the clarity I gained, I was able to make sense of my feelings and turn the writings in my journals into books and book chapters, just like this one!

5. Spend time with God. My time with God was severely compromised. One of my ex-husband's goals was to monopolize every minute of my day, including those when I was supposed to be somewhere else doing something else. When it came down to church, we would attend as a family on Sunday, but when I started going to weekly Bible study, that became a problem. When I started serving on the media team, you would have thought it was the end of the world. Although I wanted to read and study more, every time I would try to, something would interrupt. During 2020, I started a thing I call "Coffee with Jesus." I would wake up 30-60 minutes before I needed to do things, work, family, whatever, and I would spend time writing, reading, and praying. This is not the same as "me" time or journaling time. This is a specific time spent hearing from and talking to the Father. I needed guidance. I wanted to stop the whirlwind of things. I needed to quiet myself and my soul. In the busyness of life, we often forget to spend time with the one who gave it to us. It's His breath

in our lungs. He would love to spend time with us, loving on us and imparting information.

    I get it, each of these has a level of "Ugh, I can't do that." We're moms, the parents who are most present, doing all the school and extracurricular activity things, doing laundry, cooking dinner, and working full-time, part-time, anytime—when do I have time to do any of this?! I'm right there with you, and I've said the same thing. What's important to remember and what I remind myself of daily is that if I'm not "fine," my children won't be either. For far too long, we were probably in spaces and places that did not allow us to pay any attention to ourselves. In going through this process, it's easy to focus on everyone and everything else. You don't have to do them all at the same time or in numerical order. I'm a math teacher, numbered lists are my thing! Start with one thing, work through the list, and feel free to add your own things. If I could offer one piece of advice, it would be to start with #5 first. I can't remember the order I initially did, but I do know that I did not start with #5. Once I incorporated it, the other four became easier. These things are ongoing. They're new habits of life. If I knew then what I know now, I would not have leaned on my own understanding, thinking I could do any of this within my own strength and power.

Next Steps

Before we make our new beginnings declaration together, I'd like to invite you to check out my website or social media pages for encouragement, resources, and more. Self-care is a must; coming in second to that is community. I had to rebuild my friend base as I was coming out of my marriage. I'd love to be your friend. Are you ready to make our declaration? Let's go!

Declare with me: "I am no longer willing to pour from an empty cup. With the help of the Lord, I will healthily refill myself while riding through this storm. In Jesus' name, Amen."

Chapter 5

The Journey of Lament in Divorce: Navigating Pain and Healing in Psalm 31

By Amy L. Boyd

"I HAVE BEEN DEPRIVED OF PEACE; I HAVE FORGOTTEN WHAT PROSPERITY IS. THEN I THOUGHT, 'MY FUTURE IS LOST, AS WELL AS MY HOPE FROM THE LORD. ... YET I CALL THIS TO MIND, AND THEREFORE I HAVE HOPE: BECAUSE OF THE LORD'S FAITHFUL LOVE WE DO NOT PERISH, FOR HIS MERCIES NEVER END. THEY ARE NEW EVERY MORNING; GREAT IS YOUR FAITHFULNESS!
LAMENTATIONS 3:17-18, 21-23 (CSB)

My husband said he was leaving, but he hasn't. He said our marriage is over, but I don't believe it. I decided to make his favorite steak fajitas—then he will stay. This will work. As I push my cart through the small store, I greet our youth group teens who work there. I say nothing about our marital status and pretend that all is well. I actually believe it at this moment. I am the youth pastor's wife, after all.

Several hours later, he arrives home, and I am standing over hot pans filled with steak and sizzling tortillas, wiping sweat from my forehead. The smell has drawn our curious dog Molly to the kitchen, and she sits on my foot looking up expectantly, but in vain.

My husband noisily drops his oodles of keys down on the table and steps up right behind me like he always does, but he doesn't hug or kiss me. His face is so close to mine, I *almost* feel his stubble against my cheek.

"Steak fajitas?" he says questioningly as he backs away.

He looks so tired— and unusually serious. Older. Sadder. Different. Is that a gray hair near his temple?

I ignore his distant look and his perplexed tone and reply in a voice that's a bit too high and pinched, "Your favorite."

Silently, we eat fajitas in front of the TV. I study his face for signs of change. I'm sure any minute he will grin his broad smile and all will be right again. That's all it would take, just one smile. Instead, he avoids my gaze. One fajita, two fajitas, three fajitas. TV commercials blare in the background. Normally, I would demand he mute them, but today I say nothing.

Suddenly, with large, quick steps, he deposits his plate in the sink with a loud *clang*. The sound vibrates in my ears, and I jump. I wonder if the plate has broken. He strides upstairs without a word. I trudge to the sink and begin to rinse the dirty dishes as the hot water burns my fingers. It's the only logical feeling in my body: burning fingers. The sensation tethers me to my body momentarily.

The weight of circumstance pushes down on my shoulders until I sink to the floor, my back against the cabinets, the water still running, and I sob. My face is flat on the newly laid laminate flooring in our perfect house. Molly begins to lap up the pool of tears that has formed around me as she comes close, sensing my despair. I ask God, "How is this possible? I've done everything right, God, I don't deserve this. I don't know how to deal with pain like this."

Suddenly, my best plan seems so silly; the fajitas aren't *that* good. They were never going to fix whatever this is. *Had I actually thought fajitas would save the day?*

That night, I watched him sleep for hours by the flickering light of the muted TV. The relaxation in his face creates a deep ache in my heart. He is still in there, somewhere. I gently touch his shiny, dark sideburns and feel his stubbly chin. I memorize every bit of his dark eyelashes and eyebrows framing his long face. I envy his olive skin. Even with all of the hurt, this husband of mine is precious to me. "*God save this marriage,*" I pray aloud into the darkness, wondering if anyone hears me.

Following the steak fajitas attempt, he began sleeping in our basement. The days begin to blend together like a rom-com montage when it looks like the two characters actually won't end up together. Sad, cheesy music plays over them as they start to live separate lives and contemplate what life will be like without the other.

Every night, my queen-sized bed feels endless as I curl up in a fetal position on one side and the gravity of my broken world washes over me again. I shake with silent sobs. Is this how it feels when your husband dies? When is your life over?

The words of Psalm 6 (CSB) run through my mind. David calls out to God in his desperation.

> Be gracious to me, Lord, for I am weak; heal me, Lord, for my bones are shaking. (v. 2)
>
> Turn, Lord! Rescue me; save me because of Your faithful love. (v. 4)
>
> I am weary from my groaning; with my tears, I dampen my bed and drench my couch every night. My eyes are swollen from grief ... (v. 6-7a)

Weary and spent, I am dizzy as this alternate world spins all around me. What can I do? I resolve to make him see me. To force him to look me in the eye and tell me this is really and truly happening. *God, give me the right words to say to change his mind.*

When he arrives home from work the next day, I ask him point blank, "Are you *really* doing this?"

Untying his shoes, ready to bolt for the basement, he quickly looks up in surprise at my blunt question. "Yes," he states in a matter-of-fact way that alarms me more than the word itself.

I lunge at him like a bull after a red flag has been dangled and begin punching and hitting him with my tiny, powerless fists. "Why are you doing this? You **can't** do this! I won't **let** you!" I yell, and punch, and kick, and cry. The look of horror on his face confirms that I have achieved my goal. He sees me. He hears my anguish. My desperation. He cannot ignore me.

When I finally tire of jumping and flailing around to no effect, I turn and flee straight out the front door. I sit on the edge of the driveway, out of breath and out of hope. He does not follow. I cannot compel him to console me as he has for so many years. *When your loved one no longer comforts you, what does that mean?* I clutch gravel in my hands tighter and tighter to feel the pain in my body that I feel in my soul. *God, what now? My bones shake, my eyes are swollen from grief ...*

I'm not sure how long I've been crying by the side of the road. Long enough to notice stars shining overhead, and the chill of the April air has given me goosebumps. Long enough to realize my most valiant efforts are waning. Sighing, I drop the handful of rocks I have been holding, satisfied to see the tiny red specks of blood. I pull myself up off the damp driveway, brush the dirt off my jeans, and reluctantly go inside.

The basement door is ominously shut. Molly alone waits for me at the foot of the stairs, uncertainly wagging her tiny tail, and trotting behind as I ascend the stairs, away from my husband.

I can't sleep.

Knowing he is under this roof, but not in arm's reach, causes a painful ache deep in my bones and a tightness in my chest. I can't tell if I am even taking full breaths anymore. I can't be apart from him for one more second. I begin to creep down the stairs, drawn to whatever is left. After thirteen years, he can't decide that our marriage is over. Can he? *God be near.*

At the bottom of the stairs, I push against the closed door, but it only opens a foot or so. I push harder. Something is blocking the door. I stick my head through the small space and see a mini-barricade of boxes. He is sitting on the edge of the bed. Moonlight surrounds his wide eyes. I scared him. He blocked the door in fear. *He is afraid of me?*

Upon this realization, we make eye contact and begin to laugh for the first time in ages. We continue to laugh, considering the idea that I am a threat to him. That I could cause him harm, all four feet eleven inches of me, or that his little stack of boxes would keep me out. The absurdity of this moment is not lost on either of us, and we laugh from deep down within.

I sit down on the edge of the bed and put my head on his shoulder. Tears slide down my nose onto his white t-shirt as I continue to laugh. I can smell his apricot face scrub, his damp hair. His face near mine causes me to cry even harder. I reach up and touch his soft sideburns with my thumb.

Can't he feel this too? The relationship we have worked to build over all of these years? We aren't impossible to fix. We aren't past the point of no return.

"Don't do this," I whisper into the darkness.

"I have to," comes his almost indiscernible response with a large catch in his throat. We both cry sitting on our extra twin beds pushed together in our basement, and then I will myself back up two flights of stairs and fall into a restless sleep. *If I'm not his wife, who am I? God, I'm no one without him, what will I do? My tears dampen my pillow ...*

He leaves our home for good the following weekend while I am visiting my family for Easter. With my toes digging deep into my pink childhood carpet, I see a single text from him on my phone.

"I guess I won't be here when you get back."

Panic, shock, and fear jolt through my veins like I've been hit with an adrenaline shot, and I begin to shake from head to toe. I gasp aloud. I am getting divorced. I see two very clear paths ahead of me. One *with* God and one without him. How to proceed?

Immediately, I cry out in anguish—"*God help me!*" What followed were utterings that only the Spirit could understand. Confusion, desperation, and fear explode from my mind as I am unable to coherently verbalize this torrent of emotions. Again, the Spirit whispers words from Psalm 6, and I begin to repeat them over and over again, knowing I am not alone as I move forward in this new, unwanted life.

The Lord has heard my plea for help; the Lord accepts my prayer. (CSB, v. 9)

The Lord has heard my plea for help; the Lord accepts my prayer.

Entering Into Lament

The Holy Spirit had begun the work of biblical lament in me, even though I didn't know it at the time. Devouring Psalms every day gave voice to what I was experiencing and kept the lines of communication open between God and me. I desperately clutched the hem of his cloak, fearing that if I let go, I would disappear forever. Raw and unfiltered, the psalmist's language gave me the permission I needed to tell God exactly what I was feeling. *God, this is unbearable. I'm wasting away. My tears soak my bed. BE near. Why are you allowing this? How long, God?*

To contend with God was to keep grasping the broken fragments of the faith I had professed for so long, but perhaps never truly lived out. The church tradition I grew up in taught me it was dangerous to engage with your emotions. To lament was to show a lack of trust in God and his promises, but reading these lament Psalms seemed to lead to transparency with God and allowed healing to begin in a way I hadn't experienced before. Perhaps you have experienced this push and pull between what you once thought was true about who God is, and who he shows himself to be in the darkest times of your life.

In his book, *Dark Clouds, Deep Mercy*, Mark Vroegop describes lament as "a prayer in pain that leads to trust."[2] The first step in his lament process is to *turn*. Intentionally turning to God allows our lament to be focused in the right direction, towards a loving, all-knowing God. He will not turn away but we must decide that he is the direction we seek to go. When everything is upside down and backwards, and you can't help but run to the bathroom every ten minutes to cry, or scream just to make noise in your empty house, turn to Jesus.

While the initial choice to turn to God and engage with him may not be difficult, the act of turning again and again is not so easy. The inclination to rely on our own strength will take over if we aren't intentional about the honest communication that is required in the lament process. Giving voice to what we find impossible to even articulate can be the catalyst for our healing to begin. Telling God, "*I don't think I can do this for one more minute,*" places our trust in him to help us survive. Whispering into the silence, "*Jesus, Jesus, Jesus,*" as you remind yourself to keep breathing, gives the strength you need to engage in tasks you never imagined,

---

2   Mark Vroegop, *Dark Clouds, Deep Mercy* (Wheaton: Crossway, 2019), pp. 28-29.

such as finding a lawyer, opening a new bank account, or determining where you will live on your own.

May Young defines biblical lament in her book, *Walking with God Through the Valley*, as "ultimately an act of faith" that "encourages us to press in and engage God even in our brokenness and despair."[3] Biblical lament is what helps us combat the instinct we have to flee from God or push him away during times of difficulty. Adam and Eve chose to hide from God in the garden instead of facing the complicated emotions that came as they ate the forbidden fruit and fell to Satan's deception. Turning away from God is in our nature. Engaging with God is something we must intentionally cultivate, especially when we're vulnerable to walking away from God permanently.

Amidst separation and divorce, we can easily attempt to avoid lament. Admitting the loss is real means coming face to face with a future we don't want. Living a life I never imagined, feeling disoriented and uncomfortable in my own skin, was par for the course. Falling apart in a puddle of tears at the bank as I requested a copy of my statements wasn't something I wanted to do, but understanding my financial state was a reality I had to face. Finding a lawyer I could trust took more mental clarity than I possessed. Vulnerably, I had to seek the advice of friends when I wanted to keep my circumstances private. Surreal didn't even begin to describe how these days felt, but lament gave me an outlet to process these emotions *with* God.

---

3 May Young, *Walking with God Through the Valley: Rediscovering the Purpose of Biblical Lament* (Downers Grove: InterVarsity Press, 2025), p. 5.

Lament also lends itself to accepting that we are not in control. Not even a little bit. Nothing we think we have control over is actually controlled. When the curtain is lifted and we realize control is an illusion, the shock is all-consuming. You've been there, living each day as if you were perfectly in control, only to succumb to reality in one crushing revelation? Avoiding Biblical lament makes sense in many ways, but it was the single most important process to the binding up of my wounds in a way only God could accomplish.

Binding our wounds is an invisible, Holy Spirit-led process that I've been able to see in hindsight as I've moved forward in ways I couldn't imagine at the time of my divorce. Moving to another state, buying a home, and getting another dog on my own are all events I couldn't foresee in the depths of the pit. If you're caught in the depths, please know that space won't last forever. In the valley, there seems to be no escape, but God opens doors and brings new life in ways that will both surprise you and bind you to him in a reciprocal relationship that gives peace in ways a marriage relationship never could. This I know is true; by the grace of God, you're going to keep moving forward as you intentionally process this pain with God. Things will get better, I promise!

Psalm 31 provides a space to practice the components of lament as we acknowledge we are not alone, we are heard, and God is still on the throne. David wrote this psalm in a time of deep distress; possibly as he fled from Saul, who sought to kill him. David lived on the run for eight years fearing for his life, which could have resulted in his need for lament as he grieved the life he thought God had promised him and the uncertainty of his future.

By combining the lament methods of Vroegop and Young, I have found the following 5 steps useful to processing a lament Psalm along with our emotions throughout separation, divorce, and beyond:

1. Turn to God
2. Be Completely Honest
3. Affirm Who God Is
4. Shift Thinking from Fear to Faith
5. Hope for the Future

1. Turn to God

"LORD, I seek refuge in You; let me never be disgraced. Save me by your righteousness. Listen closely to me; rescue me quickly. Be a rock of refuge for me, a mountain fortress to save me. For you are my rock and my fortress; You lead and guide me for your name's sake. You will free me from the net that is secretly set for me, for you are my refuge. Into Your hand I entrust my spirit; You have redeemed me, LORD, God of truth." Psalm 31:1-5 (CSB)

The Hebrew word for LORD here is "Yahweh", meaning God's personal, covenantal name that he uses to signify his relationship with his people. This God is ever present and always keeps his promises. In Exodus 3, God reveals this name to Moses when he says, "I AM WHO I AM" as he instructs Moses to let the people know that Yahweh is with them and he **can** be trusted. When we have lost trust in the person we trusted the most, the I AM is always a trusted refuge.

The covenant God made with his people is not a one-sided agreement, but a relational commitment God makes with us. He will be our God, and in return, we will be his people. This is the Lord we seek refuge with in Psalm 31. A God who will never let us down or shame us, regardless of how much shame we feel facing divorce.

2. Be Completely Honest

> *"Be gracious to me, LORD, because I am in distress; my eyes are worn out from frustration—my whole being as well. Indeed, my life is consumed with grief, and my years with groaning; my strength has failed ... and my bones waste away ... I am dreaded by my acquaintances; those who see me in the street run from me. I am forgotten; gone from memory like a dead person—like broken pottery."*
> Psalm 31:9-12 (CSB)

Giving voice to our true feelings is how lament can help us move forward and avoid becoming stuck in self-pity. God knows our thoughts before we think them, so voicing them is no surprise. Just as my closest friends went home with tear-soaked laps during my separation and divorce period, so we must lay out our truths before God, knowing he can handle our truth.

David is consumed with grief, as if his bones are wasting away. Melting into scratchy carpet fibers on multiple occasions in unending tears, I have felt these things to my very core, crying out to God in desperation as my whole being wilts and wastes away. Several months into my separation, I saw the look on my mom's face as she took in my less than one hundred-pound frame. Tears spilled over as she saw the toll this grief had taken on my physical body. Dressing for my divorce, my clothes hung unnaturally, befitting a day I would want to erase from memory. Continually crying out,

God, how to survive the tearing of one flesh? How does one become two again?

Speaking these emotions aloud to God as we petition for an end to this despair will serve to inch us toward hope. Movement towards the light at the end of the tunnel is a purposeful quest that God is taking with us until the light warms us once again.

Taking the words right out of my mouth David exclaims, "I am forgotten, gone from memory like a dead person—like broken pottery" (Psalm 31:12, CSB). The invisible feeling of divorce was the most pronounced for me as I sought out a new church, new friends, and began an entirely new life as a broken version of myself. Fragments of my married self clung to my bones, unable to break free, securely adhered after so many years of being one. Maybe you have felt as I did that your identity was entirely shaped by being a wife, and you don't know who you are anymore. This brokenness is exactly the state God desires as he begins to shape us into who we are meant to be.

> "But the pot he was shaping from the clay was marred in his hands; so the potter formed it into another pot, shaping it as seemed best to him." Jeremiah 18:4 (NIV)

Even as David felt shunned and ridiculed by those around him, the potter was forming him into the man who would be King of Israel for more than forty years. Bringing our lament to God in plain language gives him the ability to ready us for what comes next. God has beautiful plans, and even if we want to stubbornly stay trapped in our deadened stupor, repeated lament nudges us infinitesimally in the direction of hope. Beams of light will break through the clouds in the form of a new job or a group of friends you never thought you would find as an "old," mid-thirties single.

3. **Affirm Who God Is**

"But I trust in You, LORD; I say, "You are my God." The course of my life is in Your power; rescue me from the power of my enemies and from my persecutors. Make your face shine on your servant; save me by Your faithful love. LORD, do not let me be disgraced when I call on You ..." Psalm 31:14-17a (CSB)

Lament involves reiterating who God is to us now, who he has been in the past, and who he will continue to be in the future. Claiming his promises and knowing *why* we continue to persist is a powerful way to move forward with purpose, as the direction of our lives is in his power and not our own.

His capable hands hold the course of our lives. Therefore, we are sustained by his faithful love day by day, hour by hour, minute by minute, even when things feel impossible. Even when we have to figure out how to pay bills or wash our own car, he is a personal God; *my God*, in whom I can put my full trust.

The idea that God can and will "deliver" us from our present circumstances can feel a bit vague and uncertain, but this Hebrew word (*palat*) means to rescue, save, or protect "all the way" to completion. We can trust in the timing of God's delivery and the surety of his protection because he is a loving father who will not leave us out in the cold. Providing a new home for me in an impossible, "only God" sort of way was one visible sign of obvious provision that has left me speechless at the abundance of his faithful love. He will lavishly pour his blessings upon you as well, my friend, because that is who He is.

4. **Shift Thinking from Fear to Faith**

   "How great is your goodness, which you have stored up for those who fear You. In the presence of everyone you have acted for those who take refuge in you. You hide them in the protection of Your presence; You conceal them in a shelter from human schemes, from quarrelsome tongues. Blessed be the Lord, for he has wondrously shown His faithful love to me in a city under siege. In my alarm, I had said, "I am cut off from Your sight." But you heard the sound of my pleading when I cried to You for help." Psalm 31:19-22 (CSB)

   A new perspective is beginning to formulate in our fragile hearts and minds! We don't have to be afraid of living every single moment of our post-divorce lives. As we tell God the truth and affirm who He is, our brains become wired to think in a new way. Finally believing that these circumstances won't last forever and that God is who he said he is, we can alleviate our worst fears and begin to shift our mindset to one of faithful rest. This is not to say that our circumstances will be resolved, but we have intentionally taken up a posture of trust, knowing God will be there no matter what happens.

   Even on the day of our divorce, when we may have to testify that our marriage is "irretrievably broken" and it seemed God was no longer with us, we now understand that He has always been near enough to hear us. We are not shouting out into an empty void, but crawling into the lap of our faithful father, who does not shrink away from our intensity. Our pleading has not fallen on deaf ears, but is heard by a God who does everything imaginable to protect us. No need to fear though the earth gives way and the mountains topple into the sea, God is always found in times of trouble (Psalm 46).

5. **Hope for the Future**

> *"Love the LORD, all His faithful ones. The LORD protects the loyal, but fully repays the arrogant. Be strong, and let your heart be courageous, all you who put your hope in the LORD."* Psalm 31:23-24 (CSB)

As we walk by faith through the darkness of loss, and begin to shift our thinking away from fear, we show devotion to the God who has made a covenant of love with us as we bring our lament directly to his ear. His promises ensure we can trust him with our lives. As unsettling as it is to not see what's ahead, He does.

The most well-known place in the Bible where God commands his people to "be strong and courageous" is in Joshua 1, when God is finally leading his people into the Promised Land after 40 years of wandering in the desert. While the wilderness brought many challenges, God knew the people would struggle as they entered their new space. He encourages them to persist in their faith with grit, depending on a strength that only comes from a God who knows what they face.

Just as we are thrust into a brand new life, we can dare to place our hope in Yahweh, the God who is actively engaging *in* a relationship with us. "Hope" isn't just a vague feeling or casual wish, but an expectation of God's provision and presence. Through lament, we show our confidence in the God we deliberately place our hope in, knowing that our future is secure. Life no longer looks how we thought it would, but we have peace, knowing God's plans are good because HE is good.

Lament as a Tool for Healing

Lament is one way to process our grief alongside God, knowing we are not alone and we never will be. Lament is not a one-and-done event, but a recurring spiritual practice designed to strengthen our faith during times when we can't see the way forward. God uses lament as a stepping stone along a path we can willingly walk, knowing the end is a place we want to go.

There is no set timeframe to process grief. While many well-meaning friends may imply your grief has lasted too long, lament can occur indefinitely. I will grieve this loss for the duration of my life, but the way I process and carry the grief has changed over the years. This loss is part of who I am, and intentionally bringing it with me shows that my loss had tremendous value. Lament looks different at every stage of my post-divorce life, but has continued.

Friend, it's important to remember that lament is not a vehicle for living in continual shame or depression, but a means to arrive at a hopeful, trusting place with God in spite of our circumstances. If we allow it, lament can lead to victory in who God is, and who we are becoming in him as a single woman with a beautiful purpose.

In addition to processing through Psalms, it may help to lament by writing in a journal, listening to music, taking a walk, or playing with a pet. Reaching out to trusted friends, pastoral staff, a counselor, or therapist may be a critical part of the healing process as you find words to express your unique experience.

Recalling the days of planting my tear-soaked face on the floor and aching deep down in my soul at the loss of my marriage, I can see the ways God has continued to love me so well as I came to him in honesty and trust. He wants to do the same for you, weary friend. Lament can begin transforming your heart and life to carry your loss, and step into the glorious post-divorce life God planned for you.

Written Lament for Psalm 31:

1. TURN TO GOD: Lord, I seek refuge in you; save me, listen closely to me, be a rock of refuge. You will lead and guide me because of your name. You will free me from the net that is set for me in secret, for You are my safe place. Divorce feels so scary, but you are here.

2. BE COMPLETELY HONEST: My eyes are worn out from sorrow—my whole body is spent. Grief consumes my every breath. My strength fails, my bones waste away. People avoid me out of fear that divorce will happen to them, too. I am forgotten by my husband—gone from his memory as if I am dead—shattered like broken pottery.

3. AFFIRM WHO GOD IS: But I trust you, God—you are *my* God. The course of my life is in your power alone. Your faithful love is all that helps; don't let me be disgraced as I call on you.

4. SHIFT THINKING FROM FEAR TO FAITH: I'm afraid of what will happen every day, but you are here. I felt invisible to you, too, but you heard my desperation and crushed dreams and have started to give me hope.
5. HOPE FOR THE FUTURE: Protect me. Help me to be strong and courageous and to continually put my expectations in you, embarking on a future that looks nothing like I imagined, but is still good.

Next Steps: Write Your Lament

Utilizing one of the following Psalms, follow the 5 Steps to voice your lament:

Psalm 22, 42, 13, 77, 56, 10, or 38

5 Steps:

1. TURN TO GOD:

   _____
   _____
   _____
   _____
   _____

2. BE COMPLETELY HONEST:

   _____
   _____
   _____
   _____
   _____

3. AFFIRM WHO GOD IS:

   _____
   _____
   _____
   _____
   _____

4. SHIFT THINKING FROM FEAR TO FAITH:

   _____
   _____
   _____
   _____
   _____

5. HOPE FOR THE FUTURE:

   _____
   _____
   _____
   _____
   _____

Chapter 6

Hope in Every Season: Discovering Hope, Healing, and God's Faithfulness After the Storm

By Angela King Bley

"THE LORD IS CLOSE TO THE BROKENHEARTED; HE RESCUES THOSE WHOSE SPIRITS ARE CRUSHED." PSALM 34:18 (NLT)

I recall lying flat on my bed, crying out to God, "Help me! I am drowning!"

I have a story to share with you, one that I pray brings hope if you're walking through the pain of divorce—whether it's something you're just beginning, something you're in the middle of, or something you're trying to navigate toward the end. My dear friend, I want to encourage you that if God can take a broken, messed-up woman like me and redeem my life in ways I never could have imagined, He can do the same for you. God did it for me, and He wants to do it for you, because His Word tells us He is no respecter of persons. The Bible also reminds us that our Heavenly Father desires to bless us abundantly beyond anything we could think or ask because He loves us. And friend, know this: God loves you more than you can ever comprehend

I want to be as open as I can without causing harm to my family. However, I never imagined that I would face the pain of divorce. I married someone who shared my faith, a man who was a licensed minister in the same denomination we both grew up in. We met at the annual worldwide church conference. He was visiting the college campus where I studied, and we connected through mutual friends. One specific mutual friend encouraged me to give him a chance because he was 'a good guy.' We hit it off, and despite living in different states, he in Colorado and I in Cleveland, Tennessee, we began a long-distance relationship through phone calls and letters for four months before deciding to marry. It was an unplanned elopement. My fiancé traveled to Tennessee to pick me up and take me to Colorado, his home state, where I would meet his parents. During our visit, we made the spontaneous decision to get married. While my mom was supportive of our relationship, there was tension with my stepdad, who didn't approve. In the end, we chose to elope.

From the beginning, our marriage was not built on a solid foundation. Yes, we both loved Jesus and were of the same faith. We both grew up in Pentecostal churches, just in different states. A match made in heaven. Right?! This was my guarantee of a lifelong marriage, and I was naive to believe that God would make it work because of our same background of belief. It didn't matter that I came from a dysfunctional family, where my dad struggled with his relationships with women, and my mom was often critical and controlling toward him. My parents had a turbulent marriage that ended in divorce when I was 10, but I was determined that this would not define my own life or future.

As I was saying, I never imagined the "D" word would ever be a part of my life, especially since I married a minister. I thought marrying a minister of the gospel would somehow exempt me from losing my marriage. But I was wrong. Both of us came into the relationship with baggage. We were both in love with the idea of being married and belonging to someone. I was in love with the thought of being a minister's wife, of having someone who would love and protect me. My ex-husband, I believe, was more in love with the idea of having a wife by his side as he ministered. But neither of us was truly prepared for marriage. There was no solid foundation, no deep relationship built. We united in marriage in 1985 and divorced in 2004. The devastation of our marriage coming to an end was crushing. Deep down, I had sensed it coming—my spirit stirred with warning signs, quiet red flags waving in the background, but denial settled over me like a thick morning fog: silent, heavy, and suffocating.

When the painful truth of my broken marriage finally surfaced, it struck like a gut punch, knocking the wind out of me and leaving me disoriented and reeling. I remember lying flat on my back, tears streaming, crying out to God, feeling as if I were drowning in grief and loss. Why, God? Why was this happening? Father, why couldn't You fix this? Why couldn't You cause my husband to love me the way Christ loves the church? My soon-to-be ex-husband had a deep knowledge of Scripture, studying the Bible thoroughly in preparation for his sermons. Our denomination didn't believe in divorce at the time. So, why? We had two beautiful daughters, aged fifteen and seventeen, who needed both of their parents together. Why couldn't we make it work?

My husband at the time knew the best way to love our children was to love me. I wrestled with the question: Is our marriage not worth fighting for? Why couldn't he love me like Hosea loved Gomer in the Bible? I know that free will is a precious gift from God, and I honor that. Still, deep in my heart, I held on to hope—believing that miracles were still possible. I didn't understand everything, but I chose to trust Him. God never overrides our free will, even when the choices made feel like mistakes. And regardless of the reasons, rejection is always a painful road to walk. Before the end of our marriage, I sought counseling for several months to save it, just before moving back to my home state of Tennessee as a family in 1996. I chose counseling because I wanted to restore harmony and unity. My goal was to make changes, improve communication, and foster a deeper love and understanding between us. Over time, however, we both neglected our relationship, putting everything else, including the kids' school activities, church, and family life, ahead of our marriage. While our marriage coasted along for a few more years, our bond deteriorated. Eventually, trust was lost, and with it, respect and love. When trust fades, I believe the foundation of a relationship crumbles. I knew that day had arrived, fully aware that we both contributed to the damage. We were both responsible.

No matter who is at fault, divorce hurts everyone, whether it is justified or not. Many days, the pain of divorce was greater than I could bear, and I honestly did not believe that I would survive it. I wasn't sure my children would survive it; however, God was always there for all of us. He promises in His Word never to leave us, and He gives us hope in every season, including the difficult ones. There were undoubtedly rough patches for all of us—and Lord knows, I made my share of mistakes along the way. Yet through it all, God's faithfulness never wavered. The grief lingered longer than I care to admit, but He never left my side.

They say that we grieve one month for every year of marriage. That would be nineteen to twenty months for me, and it absolutely holds true. This type of grieving is called mourning a living death for the spouse who did not die a natural death. We mourn the death of marriage. We broke a covenant made before God. I failed God, my marriage, myself, and my children. As I grieved, I couldn't shake the feeling that anyone who looked at me saw nothing but a glaring label 'D' for divorce or 'F' for failure stamped on my forehead. I struggled to understand how God could still love me or use me when I felt so lost in this pit of despair. But even in my darkest moments, God never let me go. In the midst of the pain, His presence drew nearer. The intimacy I found in Jesus became a precious refuge, and the thread of hope I clung to was the day I had invited Him into my heart as a young girl. Though my world was shaken, the foundation of prayer and God's Word that had been built in me remained steady, and my faith and hope in Him never faltered. This I know, God never wastes a hurt and will use it for His glory and our good.

In addition to turning to the word of God for strength and encouragement, I continued attending church even when I felt alone and isolated. Despite my pain, I refused to give up on Father God. My pastor, in his incredible grace and wisdom, allowed me to call his office whenever I needed to vent, and his support became a form of therapy for me. I didn't ask for permission; I simply reached out, often in the middle of the night, at two or three a.m., when waves of grief would hit. He was always there to listen (by voicemail), and during one Sunday sermon, he shared how honored he was to receive my calls, noting that it helped alleviate some of my pain and kept me from making destructive choices. He made it clear to the congregation that any one of his members was welcome to reach out anytime, reinforcing his role as a shepherd who took his responsibilities seriously.

    I knew that some way, somehow, this too shall pass. I had my faith in God, the Scriptures, my family, my pastor, and my church family, and yet I still needed more. I started attending a singles group at a church in Cleveland, Tennessee, and was told about DivorceCare. This was a lifesaver. Just as those who lose loved ones to death go through different levels of grief and mourning, so does the person going through divorce. DivorceCare is a thirteen-week group support program that gives tools for walking through the journey of divorce along with the emotions, challenges, and tools to heal. This group, along with my counselor, helped to heal my broken spirit and know that God is for me, and I do have hope for a better day! However, it is necessary to walk through the various stages of grief. On some days, I felt confident that I would get through and I would thrive again. Some days, the grief was unbearable, and all I could do was cry and cry and cry. I mean ugly cry too!

Towards the end of the thirteen weeks, I met someone through a dating service. Yes, I took that step! I was cautious not to share my address, and I met my current husband through a now-defunct phone dating program. The way it worked was simple: we communicated by leaving voicemails until we felt comfortable enough to exchange phone numbers. Eventually, we decided to meet at a restaurant of my choice. Our first meeting was quite comical. He described himself and said he'd be waiting by the front door, while I did the same to make sure he could recognize me. When I saw him, I was a little startled. He was ten years older than I, which I already knew, but it didn't bother me at all. The first thing I noticed was his long mustache that reached his chin, and his older, large Suburban. I must admit, a part of me thought, "Oh dear Lord, what have I gotten myself into?" I was guilty of stereotyping him, and I should not have. As I got to know him better, I discovered a man with quiet strength and a gentlemanly nature that swiftly captured both my attention and my heart. After 18 years of marriage, he still treats me with the same respect and kindness.

During this challenging and transitional time, I continued attending church, drawing strength from my church family, and spent months in counseling, which helped me process my own pain, understand what my two girls were going through, and figure out how to move forward. I can't say I was perfect, though. Before meeting Tom, I went out clubbing a few times, but I quickly realized it didn't bring the peace or fulfillment I was searching for. The peace I longed for could only be found in my relationship with God. That's when I met Tom, my current husband. From our first blind date, he was a perfect gentleman. We dated for two and a half years before deciding to marry. I paid attention to how he treated his mother and how he fathered his children from his previous marriage. We built our relationship on a strong friendship. He even agreed to attend church with me, and we took our time to truly understand each other. I now see how perfectly God matched me with someone who would love me deeply, who treated me like a queen, just as I had always hoped for. We've been married for 18 wonderful years, and Tom still opens doors for me, treating me with the same respect and love as he did when we first met.

In addition to marrying my best friend, I began to uncover my true dreams and aspirations. Through faith-based leadership courses led by one of our pastors at my church, I felt God stir long-dormant seeds of destiny within me. As these seeds began to grow, my confidence flourished, and I developed a strong desire to learn and accomplish more. That drive led me to return to college, where I became the first in my family to earn a degree, receiving an Associate of Arts in Business Administration.

Another priceless moment in my journey was receiving the call to ministry—a calling that still amazes me. I am deeply honored to serve Jesus and my church. While I hold the license, my husband and I understand that this calling is shared. Ministry is not mine alone; it is something we walk out together as willing vessels of the Father, committed to bringing Him glory, serving others, and offering healing where we've both experienced heartache.

Most recently, at the age of 60, I retired from my career to step into a new chapter as an entrepreneur. After working in the insurance industry since 1996, the Lord opened the door for me to become an independent insurance broker. This new venture represents both a fresh start and the fulfillment of a vision to build something of my own, with faith leading the way.

God redeemed my life and gave me more than I ever imagined. Every single day, I leaned into Father God, seeking to hear His heart for me and feel His unwavering love. With each moment, I grew stronger, and hope transformed from a distant wish to a tangible reality. Hope isn't about daydreaming of better days or longing for perfection. It's not a passive wish; hope is faith in action. It's about having boots on the ground, with each step of faith strengthening us and bearing fruit. Hope creates a plan and takes action, even when immediate results aren't visible. It's the strength to rise and move forward, even when we don't feel like it. Hope is choosing to pray and read God's Word, even when our hearts don't feel ready for it.

Hope transformed a painful season of divorce into a journey of personal growth and self-discovery in Christ. Through hope, I was equipped with the tools to rebuild my life, learn new things, and embrace the truth of how God sees me. I now have a deeper understanding of the good plans He has for me. Even amidst profound heartache, I hold fast to the truth that God is for me, and I know He is for you as well! Hope is the lighthouse that shines in our darkest moments, guiding us safely toward the destiny God has prepared for us. As the Scripture says, "For I know the thoughts that I think toward you, says the LORD, thoughts of peace and not of evil, to give you a future and a hope" (Jeremiah 29:11, NKJV).

As my husband, Tom, and I continue to embrace a life of hope and trust in God's plan for us, we recognize that our partnership, friendship, and marriage will always be a work in progress, rooted in faith. We understand that coasting or becoming complacent can be detrimental to the health of our relationship with Jesus and with each other. Marriage, we believe, is an ongoing journey to cultivate an environment of growth, forgiveness, and deep connection. We are committed to making each other a priority, continuing to date one another, but above all, we will always keep Jesus at the center, making Him Lord of all in our lives. By doing so, we trust that our marriage will be blessed and grow stronger each day.

Not long ago, I had a phone conversation with a couple in their late 80s who had been married for 70+ years. Curiously, I asked them what their secret to such a long-lasting marriage was. The husband spoke first, saying that he had loved his wife more than his own life since the day they were married. The wife happily responded that she, too, loved her husband more than her own life, but with a playful spark in her voice, she added that he was also her 'boy toy.' I couldn't help but giggle. In fact, we all shared a laugh as she explained that her husband, who was two years younger than her, kept her feeling young. Their responses warmed my heart and gave me a good laugh, but I've taken their words to heart and shared them with my husband and other couples as well.

I am thankful for God's amazing grace, He has redeemed and renewed both my life and my husband's. For over eighteen years, He has continually filled us with hope, but it all began with simple, faithful steps toward healing and restoration.

If hope feels distant and healing seems out of reach, I want to encourage you, it only takes one small step of faith at a time. Just start where you are. Begin by being honest with God. Tell Him exactly how you feel. You might as well be completely honest. He already knows, and He is not afraid of your pain, your questions, or your silence. Healing begins in that place of real and raw honesty. It did for me.

Next Steps

Each day, take five minutes of quiet time to ask, "Lord, what do You want me to know about Your love for me and the hope You offer?" Then, write down whatever He places on your heart. Let your prayer flow freely, and jot down a verse that speaks to you.

Start a journal. Use it to record your prayers, His answers, the ways your faith is growing, and the little love notes He sends your way to remind you, "I see you and I love you!" It could be a call from an old friend you hadn't heard from in years, a text message from someone who God placed on their heart to encourage you, a bird singing on your windowsill, or an unexpected card in the mail that arrives right when you need it most. These are God's whispers of love and gentle reminders that He is near you. I encourage you to look for those daily expressions of love. Write them down and treasure them. Over time, you'll begin to see your journey of hope and healing unfold—one love note, one God whisper, and one step of faith at a time.

Cry out to God. Even if all you can say is, "Jesus, help me," that's enough. He hears you and He is near to you. He is faithful to redeem, restore, and breathe new life into even the most broken places. I know this because I have lived it, and I am living proof of His faithfulness and goodness.

One last thing—if you're navigating the pain of divorce, I encourage you to seek out a DivorceCare group. It's a safe, supportive space where you can process your grief, find understanding, and take steps toward healing alongside others who truly understand. I went through it twice, and it was a pivotal part of my own healing journey. To find a group near you, visit their website at www.divorcecare.org.

Above all, never forget: God loves you more deeply than you can imagine, and He will carry you through if you let Him. He did it for me, and He will do it for you! I pray for peace and blessings to surround you as you walk this journey of healing and hope in God after divorce.

Chapter 7

A New Plan A

By Amber Brandt

> "EYE HAS NOT SEEN, NOR EAR HEARD, NOR HAVE ENTERED INTO THE HEART OF MAN THE THINGS WHICH GOD HAS PREPARED FOR THOSE WHO LOVE HIM."
>
> 1 CORINTHIANS 2:9B (NKJV)

I'll never forget how cold the tile felt under my feet as he spat out those words. "No one really likes you, Amber, they're all just pretending." This kind of harshness was usually accompanied by a drunken fit, and both were becoming more common. But while his insults often jabbed at my weight or personal style, this one hit differently. It went *identity*-deep. It was like he'd finally let me in on a joke everyone else was cackling about, but—surprise!—the punchline was me. I couldn't shrug it off as that typical, intoxicated talk he'd forget the next morning. This phrase sliced through the air like a tiny dart, lodging somewhere deep in the back of my brain. It stung when it stuck. "That's not true," I thought, attempting to shake the words loose, "... but maybe it is," a small voice whispered back.

Our relationship had been a whirlwind. It kicked up fast, quickly turned, and was over in just 2.5 years, with plenty of damage left in its wake. There had been small periods of peace and even joy sprinkled throughout, but they were short-lived, interrupted by verbal abuse, binge drinking, and countless nights spent wondering where he was. Toward the end, I also found small, curious clues in our bedroom that I tried to ignore. My worst fears later proved true. I've often referred to the day I was served papers as a "mercy killing," because who knows how long I would have held on, just trying to do what I thought was the *right* thing.

No one turns into a shell of themselves overnight. It happens slowly. Little darts chip away at you, and bigger aggressions gouge. Then one day, you wake up and barely recognize yourself anymore. Maybe you *are* a joke. If there ever was anything good about you, it has all surely oozed out of the holes by now.

Wounds like this do more than ache, they hollow you out. They bleed dry your joy, hope, and confidence. They destroy the future you had planned, leaving you buried under disillusionment, shame, and grief. Eventually, the lies completely cloud the truth of your belovedness.

It was never supposed to be this way. You promised to love, honor, and cherish each other–and *you* meant every word. So even when cracks began to show, you waved them away because every mentor you knew had promised, "Marriage is hard." But you were up to the task. Whether it was naïveté, justifying your spouse's behavior, or just plain old sincere hope, you expected it would all work out. You never anticipated your marriage would last anything short of a lifetime because you wouldn't enter a commitment any other way. So, what now?

What's left when the landscape of your future becomes an empty slate? Are you expected to spend years suffering, paying penance, exhausting yourself just trying to heal? Must you settle for a consolation prize, or whatever meager joys might come along with Plan B?

Absolutely not. And here's why: Divorce isn't your entire story—it's just a chapter—and I believe the rest of your life can still be beautiful.

I realize this may sound too good to be true right now, and that's okay. If you can't muster the strength to hope for it just yet, please borrow mine. I don't doubt it for a second, because I *know* how much God loves you. I've experienced firsthand that He's so good, He's already working on your whole New Plan A.

Embracing the Mystery

During my teens and early twenties, I believed God's will was easy to miss. He had one good, Divine Plan for my life, but it was shrouded in mystery. Finding it was like doing your taxes. Don't you dare make a mistake, but good luck figuring it out on your own. It was a tightrope, and I was blindfolded.

I spent the first few years after high school firing on all cylinders. I loved my job, I was in a great church, had an awesome community, and was growing in my faith. If it were possible to absolutely kill it in the "God's will" department, that was the closest I'd ever been. So, when this good, Christian guy unexpectedly entered the scene (and took an interest in me, of all people!), the relationship seemed to dovetail right in. There was momentum, energy, and enough shared beliefs. Turns out I was too busy looking for "signs" to notice the red flags. That spiritual intensity (that feels a little performative)? *I'm sure there's integrity under there. He's just zealous for God,* I reasoned. His preference that I wear heels instead of flats? *Dressing up does make you feel good when you think about it.* I knew God's will sometimes requires sacrifice, and I didn't mind doing things to make my husband happy. I never expected I would eventually acquiesce to everything.

Next thing I knew, I was twenty-four years old, divorced, and completely shell-shocked over how spectacularly I'd "missed" God's will for my life. But rock bottom became a turning point. When the grief finally let me up for air, I cautiously assessed what remained. Daring to peek into my little shell, I was overjoyed to find signs of life; tiny shreds of resilient, audacious hope still clinging on – gently held in place by the very love of God.

Jeremiah 29:11 (NKJV) may be one of the world's most-quoted verses, and for good reason: "For I know the thoughts that I think toward you, says the Lord, thoughts of peace and not of evil, to give you a future and a hope." But now let the promises of verses 12 and 13 sink into your bones. "Then you will call upon Me and go and pray to Me, and I will listen to you. And you will seek Me and find Me, when you search for Me with all your heart" (Jeremiah 29:12-13, NKJV).

In those early months after our final court date, these verses brought me comfort, but they also seemed like a tall order. I was calling and going and praying and seeking. I was searching for Him with all of my heart, at least the small "all" that was left. I had become little more than a shell, but if He wanted to, I would let Him move in. I would choose to trust that His plans for me were still good. Maybe they could even be great.

Over time, I slowly realized God had *never* withheld or hidden His will from me, and I had never been powerful enough to mess it up. I was relying on my own strength, squinting so hard to make out some small, elusive path, obsessing over any sign that might confirm I was doing it "right." I was sincere, but I lived in constant fear of making a mistake. I couldn't see that I was standing in the middle of a wide-open field of grace the entire time. Turns out I needed only to trust that my Guide was good, settle into His love, and keep my eyes focused on Jesus. His job was to Author my story. Mine was to relax into His lead.

Now, before we go on, let me be clear. For all this talk about how God *doesn't* withhold His will from us, I should acknowledge that He does like to hide *Himself* in unexpected places. But to be honest, He's not great at it. He always blows His cover. He tries to blend into nature, music, or the loving words of a friend, but we recognize Him easily. He simply loves us too much to stay put. He *wants* us to find him.

Healing Takes Time

After sharing about a difficult season in her own life, my mom once concluded by saying somewhat wistfully, "I don't know how God heals a human heart ... but He does." It's a bit too slow if you ask me, but I guess that's how all the most important things happen. Human gestation takes ten months. Experts say it took Michelangelo roughly four years to paint the Sistine Chapel, working fifteen to eighteen hours a day.[4] My homemade bread recipe requires a beastly twelve hours to rise. *Can you imagine!*? I'm sorry to say that even though I've been divorced for more than twenty years now, there are still little corners of my heart just now being healed. (I'm also *not* sorry to say, because what a gift it is that God's grace never quits us.) The good news is that now, when some old wound gets uncovered in me, it doesn't sting quite as much. Healing will take time, but you won't grieve forever. One day soon, goodness will tip the scale. You'll grow back to health, all marrow and sinew and lifeblood pumping. You'll return to yourself, stronger. While all this good work happens in you, there are three things I most want you to know and hold on to:

1. God sees you, and He will defend you.

We all know there are two sides to every story. The problem is when your side gets all misconstrued. It's an insult to injury. People tell lies about you, and other people believe them. Strangers jump to conclusions. No one gives you the benefit of the doubt or believes the best, and all you want to do is set the record straight. But even if you *could* sit face-to-face with every detractor, you still wouldn't be able to convince them of your perspective or intentions. I think that's one of the hardest parts of divorce (and oh, I don't know, *being human*). Dropping the fight feels like letting them win—and if you're like me, that really grinds your gears—but if you can do it, you'll give God room to work. The story of

---

4   "California Defeats Resident Work-Hour Limits." JAMA: *The Journal of the American Medical Association*, vol. 264, no. 14, 10 Oct. 1990, pp. 1788-1908.

A New Plan A

Hagar from Genesis 16 gives us a beautiful picture of what it looks like to experience God as Defender.

As the story goes, Sarai, Abram's wife, could not bear children, so she suggested he sleep with her Egyptian maid Hagar, reasoning, "... perhaps I will obtain children by her" (Genesis 16:2, NKJV). Eventually, Abram took Hagar as a second wife, and she did conceive. But then things got testy between the women, so Abram told Sarai, "'Indeed your maid is in your hand; do to her as you please'" (Genesis 16:6a, NKJV). And what apparently "pleased" Sarai was to treat Hagar harshly and humiliate her.

Understandably, Hagar fled to the wilderness and that's where the Angel of the Lord met her saying, "Behold, you are with child, and you shall bear a son. You shall call his name Ishmael [which means God hears], Because the LORD has heard your affliction ... Then she called the name of the LORD who spoke to her, You-Are-the-God-Who-Sees; for she said, 'Have I also here seen Him who sees me?'" (Genesis 16:11 and 13, NKJV). Hagar hadn't even prayed before God came to her rescue. He saw her heart and intentions, and all the injustice, abandonment, exploitation, and abuse she suffered before she could even put it into words.

Hagar may have been the first person to call God, El Roi, "The God Who Sees," but His eyes have never tired. He *saw* her, and He sees you, too. Not one silent tear or injustice toward you has gone unseen. *He* is your Defender. You need only be still and let Him work.

But what does "letting Him work" look like? It's:
- Advocating for yourself, but choosing not to retaliate out of anger.

- Letting natural consequences play out instead of trying to manipulate a situation to get the upper hand,
- Running to Jesus anytime you feel out of your depths, resting in these words from Exodus 14:13 (NKJV): "Do not be afraid. Stand still [be firm and confident and undismayed] and see the salvation of the LORD which He will accomplish for you."
- Remembering He sees it all, and He won't forget.

2. **God makes all things new.**

A few months after my divorce was finalized, I met with a former pastor and friend, Mark. I explained how much I hated feeling broken and desperately wanted to be healed. I told him I was willing to do whatever hard work I needed to ensure I didn't drag a bunch of baggage into a future relationship. He nodded reassuringly and replied, "I appreciate your willingness, and I know God will do a good, sovereign work in you. But I also want you to give yourself grace. You don't have to *do* so much. Some wounds are only healed when you're loved well. They can only be *loved out* of you."

For example, we may think we feel ready to trust again, but the rubber meets the road when we're in another relationship that requires us to try. Closeness and vulnerability tend to bring the unhealed areas to the surface. If my ex was unreliable or dishonest, I might be triggered when a new prospect doesn't call at the exact time we agreed upon. But if they consistently follow through on their promises, even one as small as a prompt phone call, it will begin to break the pattern and change the messaging. "*We're hurt in relationships, but we're healed in them, too,"* as a family friend says.

It's not that our wounds are beyond God's ability to heal instantly—nothing is—it's just that He designs relationships to rally around us. When I risk putting my trust in someone and they prove trustworthy, it heals something in me. When I risk admitting the worst to safe people—and I'm met with love and grace in return—it heals something in me. God uses people to make His love tangible ... their arms to wrap His love around us ... their words to speak His life back into us. Loving relationships fill in the gaps where trust was breached, they rewire pathways in our brain, and they overwrite our hard drives. In fact, Isaiah 43:18-19a (NKJV) says, "Do not remember the former things, nor consider the things of old. Behold, I will do a new thing." God uses His Word and the love of faithful friends to root out old lies and anxieties from the gardens of our hearts, so He can grow something new there. That's how He does His good, good work of restoration in you. That's how He makes all things new.

3. God smiles at your future.

I regularly attend a Thursday morning ladies' group at church, and recently one of our leaders, Von, pointed out something in the "Prodigal Son" story from Luke 15 that I'd never heard.

A man had two sons. The youngest one demanded his inheritance early, and the father obliged. A few days later, the son set off to a distant country where he wasted his fortune on reckless and immoral living and soon found himself destitute in the middle of a famine, forced to seek work from a pig farmer. The scripture says he was so hungry and desperate he would have gladly eaten the pig's slop and "when he came to himself, he said, 'How many of my father's hired servants have bread enough and to spare, and I perish with hunger! I will arise and go to my father and will say to him, 'Father, I have sinned against heaven and before you, and I am no longer worthy to be called your son. Make me like one of your hired servants.' And he arose and came to his father. But when he was still a great way off, his father saw him and had compassion, and ran and fell on his neck and kissed him. And the son said to him, 'Father, I have sinned against heaven and in your sight, and am no longer worthy to be called your son" (Luke 15:17-21, NKJV). The rest of the text reads almost as if the son's words went in one of his father's ears and out another (in the best way) because the dad immediately turned to his servants and ordered the planning of a huge celebration. All that mattered to the father was the return of the son.

As a child, I read myself into this story as the younger son. That whole "... all have sinned and fall short of glory of God" (Romans 3:23, NKJV) thing. As an adult and recovering good girl, I relate more to the older brother who stayed back and did what was "right," but fell into judgment and resentment over the whole thing. But what has never changed for me is understanding the goodness of the Father. That's only grown in richness as I've learned more about the cultural implications and context of how he operates in the story. For instance, did you know that when a son or daughter returned home in disgrace, the elders of the city would determine whether they could even be admitted back into the community? At the tiniest sight of his son afar off, the father took off running so he could beat the city officials to the gates. And when he did, he also saddled up his garments, exposing his legs, risking embarrassment and impropriety. These details illustrate his one objective—to welcome his boy home.

The thing I had never seen in the story until Von shared it has to do with the speech the son rehearsed and planned to deliver to his father. When the time came, the father cut him off before the big finish, "Make me like one of your hired servants." The father simply wouldn't hear of it. He had already forgiven the son and launched into celebrating his return before he could even get the words out. He was essentially telling his boy, "You don't have to grovel or debase yourself. Let's just go ahead and get to the good part."

Now, I'm not insinuating for a second that because someone is divorced, they're a "prodigal" son or daughter, or that God is in any way dismissive of your pain. His MO isn't about rushing or steamrolling us through tough things. The point is His *goodness*. The point is that the past is gone. The father wasn't dismissing his son's errors or pain; it simply wasn't worth rehashing anything that might cause shame or scorn. The details of the son's mistakes weren't worth dwelling on. There was no penance to pay, no shame to bear, no belly to crawl on. There was only the hope and joy of their future together. Would they have some stuff to unpack together? Sure. But the truest thing about the son in that moment was that he was beloved by his father.

And that's the truest thing about you, too. Everything else is swallowed up in that.

A Soft Place to Land

When I reflect on the moments that impacted me most during the implosion of my marriage and its aftermath, there's one memory that sticks out above them all. Louder than the shouting, deeper than the betrayal, more visceral than the shame, was the wordless support of my friend Laura. She took me in when I didn't know where to go. She cooked food, brewed coffee, and listened for days. Her eyes held me as I poured my heart out. I didn't know how to fix any of it, and she didn't try. Instead, she simply sat with me on the couch, witnessing the loss, holding my grief, sharing my tears, and matching my helpless shrugs ... There, sitting perfectly still, she carried me. She was Jesus to me.

And so today, as I sit on my own cozy couch, I'm doing that for you ... holding the complexity of your story, witnessing the depth of your grief, and sharing your tears ... The only difference is that Laura's support was sacredly silent, and I've yapped on for pages now. Hope you don't mind just a few more.

Wherever these words found you today, I hope they brought you a soft place to land. I hope you heard my heart saying, "You are not alone. You never were. You don't have to settle for a second-rate life when you serve a God Who promises to make beauty out of all these ashes. You're in a fresh new chapter written by the One Who is for you, the One Who only believes the best of you. May you feel the tenderness and weight of His love, and rest in the comfort of knowing He's got your future, and I know it's going to be great."

You've already faced the unimaginable. Now trust the One Who can do more than you could ever imagine.

Stepping Into the Story

I wish I could say that processing my divorce made me proficient at handling difficult relationships, but people just keep people-ing, ya know? It's still hard for me to let God work when it's so easy to take back the reins. Tit for tat feels justified. Being petty hurts-so-good. (I'm sure you can't relate.)

The truth is, a desire to control typically comes from something deeper and worth exploring. It could be unresolved anger, which James 1:20 (NKJV) reminds us, "... does not produce the righteousness of God," or maybe it's fear. If giving up control feels hard for you, too, here are some questions to consider and see what bubbles up.

1. When did you last feel the urge to be petty/retaliate? What triggered it?
2. What emotions came up in you?
3. What would happen if you didn't retaliate?
4. What does "being in control" protect you from?
5. Is it okay if you don't "win"?
6. What might God have for you in this?

Chapter 8

Uncovering the Lies of Gaslighting: How Knowing the Truth Changes Everything

By Ashley Boswell

"YOU WILL KNOW THE TRUTH, AND THE TRUTH WILL SET YOU FREE." JOHN 8:32 (NIV)

Let's face it, you've probably heard the term "gaslighting" thrown around quite a bit. But beyond the buzzword, what does it *really* mean? And more importantly, what happens when someone deliberately twists your reality, making you doubt your own sanity? Gaslighting isn't just a little white lie; it's a manipulative tactic that can range from subtle distortions to outright psychological abuse that makes you question your memories, your perceptions, and your very identity.

This insidious form of manipulation can erode your sense of worth, leaving you feeling inadequate and lost in a fog of self-doubt. But there's a path back to clarity and truth. This chapter will guide you in reclaiming your God-given identity, firmly rooted in Christ. Together, we'll dismantle the lies of gaslighting with the unwavering truth of Scripture. You'll learn to cultivate discernment through the Holy Spirit, enabling you to recognize and reject manipulative tactics. By grounding yourself in God's Word, you'll rebuild your sense of worth, understanding that another's distorted reality doesn't determine your value, but by your identity as a beloved child of God. Through prayer, biblical study, and reliance on the Holy Spirit, you will learn to trust your own judgment again, recognizing the voice of God's truth amidst the chaos of manipulation, and find healing and restoration in His unfailing love.

Comforting Lie or the Uncomfortable Truth

Outside of my counseling office, I find immense joy in training horses, including those rescued from abuse and wild mustangs. What's remarkable about horses is their inherent honesty. They present themselves authentically, clearly communicating their needs and preferences. This straightforward nature is a key reason I incorporate horses into counseling practice. They teach humans to be more direct and genuine in expressing their own feelings and needs. While horses can experience pain and trauma, unlike humans, they don't employ manipulation to get what they want. A mistreated horse might bite, kick, or buck, but these are reactions, not calculated attempts to deceive. Humans, however, can and do manipulate, often as a maladaptive coping mechanism rooted in past mistreatment, perhaps in childhood. They might project their insecurities onto others, trying to shift blame and make the other person feel like the problem.

This dynamic is where insecurity takes hold and a true sense of identity can be lost – when another person's distorted perception becomes our perceived reality, overshadowing our inherent worth in God's eyes. I recall a time when I internalized blame, constantly thinking, "If only I had done this differently, things would be better." Perhaps you recognize this feeling. As someone with strong convictions, I often left manipulative interactions feeling confused and guilty, as if I were solely responsible. If these feelings resonate with you, please know that you are not alone.

It is important for our healing to remember that our story didn't begin with someone doing something wrong to us. It began before we were born, intertwined with the history of mankind, in a beautiful garden where we fellowshipped freely with our Lord and enjoyed all of His beautiful creation. This idyllic beginning, however, was shattered by a lie, a manipulation that presented itself as truth.

The biblical account of Adam and Eve in Genesis 3:5 reveals the serpent's deceptive tactic: promising that eating from the forbidden tree would grant them godlike knowledge of good and evil, thereby targeting their cognitive abilities. This narrative of humanity's creation and subsequent fall from grace provides a foundational framework for understanding the origins of mental health issues and psychological difficulties. Before the Fall, Adam and Eve existed in perfect harmony with God and with each other. Their perception of the Lord was clear, accurate, and rooted in Truth. They possessed an intimate knowledge of the Lord, enabling them to form thoughts and attitudes aligned with His divine nature. However, this pristine state was irrevocably altered by the Fall. Adam and Eve's perceptions fractured, disrupting their harmonious relationships with God, creation, and even themselves. Their inherent trust in God was replaced by fear, a novel and unsettling emotion, leading them to hide from Him and experience shame for the first time.

As William T. Kirwan articulates in his book *Biblical Concepts for Christian Counseling*[5], this broken relationship with God resulted in specific losses. Because of the fall, every person is born with a lost sense of belonging, self-esteem, and strength. Throughout our lives, we continue to experience loss in these core areas. Furthermore, the enemy actively seeks to reopen and expose our deepest wounds, and life will inevitably present unexpected circumstances that leave us searching again for our identity. This vulnerability created by the Fall makes us susceptible to further wounding, particularly through relational trauma.

Experiencing relationship trauma can reactivate these fundamental wounds of separation. Tactics like lies, gaslighting, passive-aggressive behavior, and manipulation undermine the recipient's cognitive functions, inducing confusion and self-doubt. By distorting a person's perception of reality, they aim to maintain control, mirroring the serpent's pursuit of power through manipulated knowledge. Prolonged exposure to this kind of abuse can lead to cognitive distortions, where individuals perceive reality inaccurately. For example, gaslighting techniques—like twisting conversations or falsely claiming to have communicated information—cause a person to doubt their

---

[5] William T. Kirwan, *Biblical Concepts for Christian Counseling: A Case for Integrating Psychology and Theology* (Grand Rapids: Baker Academic, 1984).

own memory and perceptions. This self-doubt represents a significant cognitive distortion, echoing the initial deception in the Garden.

Another form of cognitive distortion that can develop in abusive relationships is romanticizing the positive aspects while minimizing or ignoring the negative ones. This tendency to cling to favorable memories, even when contradicted by reality, mirrors Adam and Eve's susceptibility to the serpent's deceptive promises. The allure of a comforting lie can overshadow the acceptance of an uncomfortable truth, both then and now, perpetuating a cycle of distorted thinking and hindering true healing.

Based on my own journey and my work counseling countless women who've experienced the pain of relationship trauma, I've learned that holding onto a familiar lie can feel far easier than confronting a difficult truth. For me, it was much simpler to believe I could fix my marriage through my own efforts than to accept that the outcome was beyond my control and required complete trust in the Lord every step of the way. I held onto the belief that our vows before God guaranteed restoration. While I know God is capable of anything, including restoring marriages, I eventually faced the reality that this wasn't always His plan, and it wasn't for mine.

During that challenging time, my faith was truly tested. I discovered that trusting God's provision and His plan for my life was often harder than clinging to the comforting illusion that I was in control. Science actually backs this up: our brains are wired to gravitate towards what's familiar, even if it's ultimately not beneficial. Think about our reliance on comfort food during stressful times – even though we know it's unhealthy, our brains seek that temporary sense of solace.

The good news is that God is here to restore our knowledge of Truth. As believers, we know our loving Father is actively restoring us to Himself. He gives us a sense of belonging, understanding of our worth, and the ability to rely on His strength. Our only job is to be a willing partner in the process.

From Broken to Belonging

The yearning for connection is fundamental to our human experience, a longing that has been present since humanity's first separation from Him. We see this poignantly in Genesis 3:7-8, where Adam and Eve, immediately after disobeying God, vividly hid in shame and guilt. Their once-perfect connection with their Creator was irrevocably fractured, a consequence that resonates throughout human history, impacting our innate sense of belonging in this fallen world.

This initial loss of connection, however, is often compounded by the relational traumas we experience within a sinful world. When someone uses manipulation to distort reality or isolation as a form of control, it severs your connection to truth and valid relationships. This breakdown of connection and validation profoundly alienates you, impacting your sense of belonging by making you feel like you are unworthy of genuine connection and unable to trust your judgment.

The impact of these experiences on our ability to trust extends far beyond our human relationships, significantly affecting our relationship with God. Shortly after I was separated from my now ex-husband, I vividly recall the prayer I prayed when he asked me to marry him. I specifically asked God if I was supposed to marry him, and if not, to redirect my heart. God responded very clearly that I was to marry him. I found this so confusing during my divorce and doubted if I had actually heard the Lord correctly. I believed that I no longer had, and maybe never had, a gauge on what was true anymore. At the time, I felt abandoned by both my husband and my Father in Heaven. The only way I could establish a baseline of truth and reconnect was to spend long periods of time resting at my Father's feet, restoring my sense of belonging by better understanding who God is as my Father.

To truly restore my sense of belonging and understanding of God's truth, two critical questions about God the Father needed answers: First, can I genuinely trust that God will care for me as a Father would, even in the most difficult situations? And second, how can I be sure that the voice I hear is truly His and not just my own thoughts? Perhaps these are questions you've also wrestled with. If you've experienced a lack of care in earthly relationships or struggled to trust due to lies and manipulation, these questions will likely feel especially relevant to your own journey.

The Lord graciously answered both of my questions with specific Bible verses. To the first question, about trusting His fatherly care in any situation, He showed me Galatians 4:4-7 (ESV): "But when the fullness of time had come, God sent forth his Son, born of woman, born under the law, to redeem those who were under the law, so that we might receive adoption as sons. And because you are sons, God has sent the Spirit of his Son into our hearts, crying, 'Abba! Father!' So you are no longer a slave, but a son, and if a son, then an heir through God." This verse revealed that even though we will inevitably face pain and sorrow in this broken world, because God sacrificed His Son for us, His children, we are no longer enslaved to sin, both our own and the sins committed against us. As His adopted children, we can have confidence in His plan, knowing we share in His inheritance and have a secure place in His eternal purpose.

Because animals, particularly herd animals like sheep and horses, have always resonated deeply with me, it wasn't surprising that the Lord answered my second question about discerning His voice through a shepherd analogy: "My sheep hear my voice, and I know them, and they follow me" (John 10:27, ESV). Just as a shepherd intimately knows his sheep, and they recognize his voice, we too can learn to recognize God's voice by cultivating an intimate relationship with Him. This intimacy develops through spending time in His Word, engaging in prayer, and learning to discern the promptings of the Holy Spirit.

Ultimately, the journey of healing from relational trauma and restoring our sense of belonging begins with reconnecting to our Heavenly Father. By understanding His unwavering love and learning to discern His voice, we can find the secure foundation of truth and belonging that earthly relationships may have fractured. He longs to restore our hearts and minds, leading us back to the secure knowledge that we are His beloved children, eternally connected to Him.

Worthy in Christ Alone

When Adam and Eve lost their sense of belonging and hid from God in the garden, they simultaneously experienced a devastating decline in their self-esteem. Overwhelmed by guilt and shame, their perception of their own worth plummeted (Genesis 3:7-10). This initial wounding, stemming from our separation from God, continues to impact us today.

This fundamental attack on our self-esteem manifests in all forms of abuse, compounding the wounds inflicted by original sin. When we endure any kind of abuse in a relationship, we often begin to question our inherent worth, and our minds can tragically accept the lie that we are unlovable.

Speaking from my own experience, I know this process of reclaiming worth is often complicated by the tendency to internalize blame, especially after experiencing manipulation in relationships. It becomes easy to turn inward and ask, "What did I do wrong to cause this?" While introspection can be valuable for understanding how to respond better to situations, it's crucial to recognize the distinction between healthy self-reflection and taking on full responsibility for another person's actions.

This tendency to assume blame is, in essence, a misguided attempt to control an uncontrollable situation. When we turn inward, we have a tendency to be overly critical and unloving toward ourselves. This is not how Jesus sees us. Our worth is not defined by us or anyone else; instead, it is defined by the one who sacrificed His life for us.

The ultimate fulfillment of our need for self-esteem is found in God the Son, Jesus Christ. His unconditional love, acceptance, and regard for us, demonstrated through His sacrifice on the cross, provide the very foundation for our sense of worth. This love, manifested in His willingness to prioritize our needs above His own, empowers us to do the same for others, even to the point of loving our enemies.

Because Jesus became fully human, He can empathize with our pain and weakness. Whatever we are going through, His victory over death means we can triumph in reclaiming our true identity in Him. Created in His image, our self-worth should reflect the immeasurable value He places upon us, for "Since you are precious and honored in my sight, and because I love you, I will give people in exchange for you, nations in exchange for your life" (Isaiah 43:4 NIV). Only God determines our worth, and Jesus solidified His love for us when He gave His life in exchange for ours.

The next time you feel unworthy of love, remember these verses from Ephesians 3:17-19 (NIV): "And I pray that you, being rooted and established in love, may have power, together with all the Lord's holy people, to grasp how wide and long and high and deep is the love of Christ, and to know this love that surpasses knowledge—that you may be filled to the measure of all the fullness of God." Notice from this verse that Christ's love covers all directions from top to bottom and left to right, including where you've been (past), where you are (present), and where you are going (future). This love also may not be comprehensible on this side of heaven, but it is not for our minds to decide and agree on this love for it to be true; instead, it is an absolute fact determined by Christ. Let Christ alone be the love barometer to your worth, and you will find an absolute amidst any earthly relationship, pain, or struggle you face.

His Strength Is Our Superpower

Humanity was initially created to feel secure and live under God's authority. In the beginning, God provided this security and leadership for Adam and Eve. However, when they desired more independence and disobeyed God's commands, the opposite happened: they lost all sense of control and security. Ever since, humankind has been trying to regain control and understand life and its events. When people feel powerless, helpless, and unable to act, depression can often result.

Adam and Eve's decision to prioritize their own desires over God's clearly shows the consequences of choosing our plans instead of His. Whenever we substitute God's plan for our own, we miss out on His best for us and risk harming ourselves and others. This is especially true for individuals who use gaslighting or other manipulative tactics. They will prioritize their own needs above everyone else's, including God's commands and promises. Driven by a strong urge to relieve their pain and satisfy their desires at any cost, they can inflict significant harm on those around them. Anyone in a long-term relationship with such a person is vulnerable to the damaging effects of their selfishness.

For anyone who is currently in or has experienced a relationship characterized by frequent manipulation, the result is often a profound loss of control and security. The path to healing for the victim begins with the crucial step of allowing the Holy Spirit to have the ultimate authority in their life. Only the Holy Spirit possesses the ability to speak directly to our entire being – our mind, our will, and our emotions – in a way that brings true healing and provides lasting security.

As humans, we are uniquely created by God as spiritual beings, setting us apart from all other forms of His creation. We possess a triune nature: body, soul, and spirit. Our physical form is the body; our intellect, emotions, and will reside in the soul; and our spirit is our life force, directly given to us by God. While animals also have a body and a soul, the spirit is exclusive to humanity, making us a distinct and special part of God's creation. Understanding this spiritual dimension is essential in recognizing how we can rediscover the security and loving guidance we deeply long for.

The Holy Spirit, God's very presence living within believers, is our source of strength to obey the Lord and overcome life's difficult situations. Consider the Holy Spirit as your divine superpower! As part of the Trinity, He guides our choices, shields us from spiritual harm, and offers comfort and hope when we are afraid. Just as Jesus promised in John 14:26 (NIV), "But the Advocate, the Holy Spirit, whom the Father will send in my name, will teach you all things and will remind you of everything I have said to you." [1] Knowing that He would be leaving, Jesus sent the Holy Spirit to be our wise counselor and leader. The more time we spend in God's presence and immerse ourselves in His Word, the better we will be able to recognize the Holy Spirit's guidance and follow His plan for our lives.

The Greek word "Parakletos" used in this passage is translated in various ways, such as Comforter (KJV), Helper (ESV), and Advocate (NLT). These translations beautifully illustrate the additional roles the Holy Spirit fulfills in providing the comfort and security we so desperately need. By releasing our need for control and allowing the Holy Spirit to lead us, we can rediscover the security and benevolent leadership that was lost in the Garden of Eden, ultimately finding true rest and direction in God's loving presence.

The Lord has an ongoing desire to connect with our spirit. Before humanity's fall into sin, Adam experienced direct spiritual communion with God because he was in perfect fellowship with Him. However, after the Fall, Adam's spirit became separated from God. Ever since, our human spirit struggles to fully connect with Him, and we often try to fill this spiritual emptiness with worldly things instead of God. This leaves us feeling empty and often leads to hopelessness as we search for solutions or comfort in the world to soothe our fears. Our natural tendency might be to engage in "retail therapy" or to immerse ourselves in activities like my horse training for extended periods. Others might overindulge in eating or drinking. Ultimately, none of these things can truly satisfy our spiritual longing; only the Holy Spirit can.

Our goal in spiritual recovery from relationship trauma is to strengthen our spiritual capacity so that we can clearly hear and receive hope and healing directly from the Lord, rather than relying on temporary, worldly fixes. Once we can clearly discern our Lord's voice, we must then actively choose to obey His leading, aligning our will with His, for "the Spirit God gave us does not make us timid, but gives us power, love, and self-discipline" (2 Timothy 1:7 NIV).

A crucial initial step in obedience is identifying harmful patterns in our own behavior and in the actions of those around us. Recognizing these patterns allows the Holy Spirit to guide us in setting healthy boundaries for our protection. After my divorce, I personally experienced a destructive pattern of constant vigilance, always anticipating the next problem or expecting something painful or negative to occur. This feeling might resonate with you, especially if you've been in a relationship where the truth was often hidden, leading to unexpected shocks. Over time, by immersing myself in God's promises and memorizing scripture, I gradually began to recognize these fearful, intrusive thoughts and intentionally replace them with God's truth. The Holy Spirit was instrumental in helping me identify these lies and recall the alternative truth found in God's Word. Even now, I continue to rely on the Holy Spirit to reveal any lies I need to replace with His truth.

Now, I invite you to join me in allowing the Holy Spirit to be your strength in this process of recognizing and overcoming harmful patterns. This is a call to action: take a close look at your own heart and the circumstances you are facing. Where are you prioritizing the desires of others, including your own selfish desires, over God's will? And where are you allowing yourself to experience harm? Please understand that setting boundaries is not selfish or ungodly; rather, it is an act of self-preservation and an act of obedience to God's desire for your well-being. Make the conscious choice today to surrender to His will, trusting that His strength, which is renewed as you choose obedience, will empower you to break free from these damaging patterns and walk in the fullness of His intended purpose for you. This includes the strength to say "no" when necessary. Embrace the promise found in Isaiah 40:31: "But those who hope in the Lord will renew their strength. They will soar on wings like eagles; they will run and not grow weary, they will walk and not be faint" (NIV). Allow the strength He provides to lift you up, knowing that His deepest desire is for your healing and protection.

The Foundation for Reconstruction

In the aftermath of relationship trauma, the path to healing lies in reclaiming our true identity. After the shattered pieces of glass, our fractured self-perception demands reconstruction, not with the lies we've been told, but with the unwavering truth found in Christ.

It is in Him that we discover our belonging, worth, and strength, not defined by the actions of others, but by His enduring love. This chapter has illuminated the nature of deception and its power to erode our sense of self. Yet, it also points to the ultimate antidote: a foundation built on the unshakable truth of God's Word, a truth that dismantles lies and restores our fractured selves, offering a profound and lasting peace.

Now, the critical question becomes: how do we actively translate this understanding into tangible healing? It is in seeking divine guidance and embracing the tools God provides that we begin to reconstruct our identity, piece by shattered piece. It is time to deliberately confront the lies that have defined us and resolutely embrace the truth that sets us free.

To begin this process of reconstruction, we must first identify the specific lies that have taken root in our understanding of who we are. These lies can stem from external sources, like hurtful words from others, or internal sources, like distorted beliefs about ourselves in relation to God and the world. This includes the limiting titles you have assigned yourself or accepted from others. For example, some of you who are mothers may believe you are "only a mom," not permitting the belief that you are truly children of God, unable to accept His unconditional love. By bringing these lies into the light, we open ourselves to divine revelation and begin the journey toward healing. After spending time with the Lord, reflecting on these questions, write your responses below:

- What is the relationship between God's truth about your identity and your personal beliefs about yourself?
- How does God's definition of who you are influence what you believe about yourself?

Next, consider what role God's Word plays in your life. Is it your primary guide? Is it solely for those around you, or is there a broader calling for you to engage with it deeply?

Think honestly about where you are positioning yourself in relation to others. Maybe you think you should be further along in some areas. If you find a clue about where you believe you stand in life, pay attention to when you compare yourself to others or use 'should' phrases when talking to yourself. These comparisons and 'shoulds' often reveal underlying lies about your worth and progress.

Finally, consider how you are functioning in your daily life. Are you relying solely on your own strength to navigate your challenges and make decisions?

Are you allowing others to dictate your choices and determine your path? Recognizing areas where you are operating outside of God's truth and relying on your own limited understanding is a powerful step toward allowing His truth to guide you.

Take heart, dear reader. The journey of rebuilding your identity on the solid foundation of God's truth is a courageous one, and you are not alone. As you actively engage with these questions and invite God's perspective into your understanding of yourself, you will begin to dismantle the lies that have held you captive and step into the fullness of the person He created you to be. Embrace this process with hope and trust, knowing that God's unwavering love is the ultimate architect of your true and beautiful identity.

My deepest hope is that you find complete healing after the pain of relationship trauma and come to see yourself as God sees you: as a beloved child within your Father's family, empowered by the Holy Spirit to reclaim everything that was lost, both now and for eternity.

Chapter 9

Wholly Broken, Wholly Restored: How God Can Turn Our Pain into Purpose

By Stephanie Lauren Jordan

> "... EACH OF US HAS THE OPPORTUNITY TO THRIVE IN SITUATIONS WE NEVER DREAMED WE'D HAVE TO EXPERIENCE."[6]
> KATHERINE AND JAY WOLFE

Anger flooded my veins while uncertainty consumed my every thought. Fear and grief had already begun rewiring my brain as the words came out of my then-husband's mouth, "I don't want to do this anymore. I would be happier alone." Like a knife, those words pierced my heart.

After years of friendship and then years of dating, we were only married a year when my husband left because he felt he wasn't ready for marriage. Divorce was not something I ever wanted, nor was it something I ever anticipated happening in my life. As a child of divorce, I was determined

---

[6] Katherine Wolf and Jay Wolf, *Suffer Strong: How to Survive Anything by Redefining Everything* (Grand Rapids: Zondervan, 2020), p. 17.

that that would never be a part of my journey. But, almost as quickly as we started married life, it was over.

It wasn't just the end of a marriage; it felt like the end of my life. All the hopes, dreams, and plans we had were now washed away. What would I do? How would I cope? Was there any chance of being loved again? I was completely, utterly, *wholly broken*.

One week after my marriage ended, in March of 2020, the United States went into lockdown for COVID-19. Talk about adjusting to a new life ... After living through the pandemic, we all started to refer to certain moments in life as "pre-COVID" and "post-COVID". It was a crisis that so radically changed our lives that we gave it its own timeline. Divorce can have the same effect on us. It changes our lives in such a way that it feels like "pre-divorce" was one life and now "post-divorce" is another. And honestly? It's true.

You don't physically become a new person, of course, but your life will never be the same again. That might be terrifying to hear. Years ago, it wasn't something I could admit or accept about myself because I didn't want a new life. I prayed for marriage restoration and desperately wanted things to go back to normal, but that life was over.

You're likely reading this book right now because you've been through a divorce, too. You're facing the daunting reality of a new life while trying to alleviate the feeling of irreparable brokenness. If I can offer some hope: It doesn't have to feel like this forever. This new life doesn't have to be something to dread or wish away. Your brokenness doesn't have to destroy your future. If we were able to create a new normal post-COVID, then we can also create a new normal post-divorce.

It wasn't apparent right after my divorce—pain has a way of filtering our perspectives—but God had a beautiful new life in store for me. I just had to be willing to see and consider what I hadn't before. For all of us, once we can see our brokenness through a new perspective, it will change the way we suffer and propel our journey to healing.

Perspective shifts are pervasive in Scripture, particularly through the teachings of Jesus. Christians are called to serve others in humility, as opposed to serving our self-gratifying nature (Matthew 20:26-28, Luke 14:11, and Philippians 2:3-4). We also have a responsibility to love and forgive our enemies, not cancel them or curse them (Matthew 5:43-44 and Romans 12:20-21). We're told that it's in death that we find abundant, eternal life (Colossians 3:3, Mark 8:35, and John 12:24). And, my personal favorite, we learn that pain and brokenness can actually become the means by which we are made whole (Matthew 5:3-4,10 and James 1:2-3).

The Kingdom of God is an upside-down, inside-out Kingdom that challenges the way we see the world and, subsequently, shapes the way we live. This makes some areas of life tougher (like loving our enemies), but it also offers us a hope like nothing else can. One such hopeful encouragement comes from the Apostle Paul in the book of Romans.

"And we know that God causes everything to work together for the good of those who love God and are called according to his purpose for them." (Romans 8:28, NLT)

Over the next few pages, I'd love to share with you how God used this verse to give me hope and insight while He walked with me through divorce, and how He can do the same for you.

The Good, The Bad, and The Divorce

It's no secret that every human faces hardship and heartbreak at some point. It could be a divorce or the death of a spouse. It could be the loss of a parent or a child. Maybe it's financial issues, mental or physical health struggles, or being a victim of oppression and injustice. (Of course, we'll likely deal with a combination of these, and others, over a lifetime, not just one of them.) Life is certainly no walk in the park.

Despite knowing this, there's always a part of us that expects to get through life unscathed. We pray for the perfect marriage, good kids, a job we love, financial blessing, health and longevity, and loyal friends–i.e., an easy life. And when any one of those gets touched with hardship, we are left in shock. Don't get me wrong, I don't think it's bad to want a life full of good things, but we must not be naive to the existence of suffering in this life.

Christians, in particular, struggle with this. We believe God to be good, loving, and all-powerful; so why would He ever let anything bad happen to us, His beloved children? Why would He let a spouse walk away and leave our lives shattered? It doesn't seem to line up with what we believe or what we expect. While God does promise an ultimate deliverance and redemption from suffering and evil one day (Revelation 21:4), He doesn't promise that we will be free of it while on earth (John 16:33). Paul reiterates this truth in his letter to the Romans. Life is full of pain, but that doesn't mean God can't use that pain for better purposes.

At the end of the day, the Christian life is not about figuring out how to avoid suffering; it's about learning how to deal with it. This takes acceptance and adaptation. We still grieve the pain and loss in our suffering, but we also accept the realities of the situation. There is no going back in time to change or avoid what happened, and there are elements involved that are beyond our control. Acceptance means recognizing that life *will* be different moving forward, and this paves the way for adaptation. When we are willing to accept our situation, we can adapt by pursuing and embracing the opportunities available to us for growth and healing. But there's something truly incredible about suffering in the life of a Christian, and it is this: we have a God who steps in and does something about it! He is not a passive observer of our suffering.

"And we know that **God causes everything to work together for the good** of those who love God and are called according to his purpose for them" (Romans 8:28, emphasis added). That is: God uses every bit of our lives–our successes and our failures, our faithfulness and our unfaithfulness, our joy and our pain–as a contribution towards good. He deals with our suffering not by erasing it but by redeeming it. And there is nothing we go through that He can't use!

Now, this does not suggest that we start believing that all things *are* good. Abuse, injustice, oppression, sickness, poverty, and other kinds of evil or suffering are not good things. This verse is not about calling what's bad good; rather, it's about seeing how God can use the bad for the purpose of good. In the midst of heartbreak and grief, God is already at work behind the scenes to bring about something beautiful.

Like an artist creating a mosaic, God sees the broken parts of us as integral pieces to the masterpiece He's creating for our lives. He doesn't do it reluctantly or out of obligation, He does it out of His genuine love and goodwill towards us. We can accept and adapt to our pain and suffering because we know what God can do with it. The good, the bad, and, yes, even the divorce can ALL be used by God for good.

Defining "Good"

It's hard to believe that anything good can come from such pain after a divorce. I remember questioning God on the matter: "Why are you letting this happen? Aren't you the world's biggest supporter of marriage? What good can possibly come of this?" I prayed fervently that God would restore our marriage because I genuinely thought that was the "good" He wanted. A marriage that reflected forgiveness and redemption and gave God glory. What better outcome is there? But our marriage wasn't restored, and I've come to be grateful for that. God has done so much more good through my divorce than I ever thought possible, but to truly see all the good He's done, I had to learn what "good" means in the context of the Christian life and faith.

Think for a minute about how you would define "good". Is it similar to this? – A material or circumstantial blessing that benefits the life of the recipient; the resolution, avoidance, or absence of bad; to receive what one desires. For me, when I look at Romans 8:28, these tend to be the definitions I have at the forefront of my mind. To know that God will work things together for my good sends my thoughts straight to "Ohhh yes, I'm going to get what I want!" Unfortunately, this same mindset leaves many Christians discouraged and angry at God when we don't actually receive what we want. But, giving us what we want is not really God's M.O. It's not that our wants are completely corrupt (though, of course, they can be at times). It's that we sometimes just don't know any better. God knows that what we want is often not what we need, or it's not the best possible version of what we need.

In the midst of divorce, our wants can be driven by our pain and can become narrowly focused on the immediate resolution of that pain. We can have a simplistic, surface-level view in believing that what is good is whatever relieves our suffering and makes us happy in the moment. However, God has a much deeper definition of what is good. He has the ability to see beyond our emotions, beyond our present circumstances, and know what is best for us.

As I said, in my own divorce, I simply wanted God to give me my marriage back. But He knew what was better for me, for others, and for His Kingdom. Here are a few examples, as an encouragement to you, of some of the greater good that came from my divorce:

- A deeper relationship with God that brought peace, hope, joy, and love like I'd never experienced before.
- Opportunities to reflect on the situation, learn from any mistakes, and grow in wisdom.
- It created a connection point with a close friend who had also gone through a divorce. She decided to attend church and came to know God's love in her own life.
- As I've shared my story publicly, others have been able to find comfort and healing and grow in their faith.

- I'm now newly remarried; it has brought unconditional love and continues to refine me for the better.

None of these were outcomes I foresaw, because I had a limited perspective on what good meant. But God opened my eyes and showed me all the good that He could bring from my pain and brokenness.

There's a common denominator at the root of any good that God brings about in our lives. We see it in the latter part of Romans 8:28 (NLT), "... for the good of those who love God and are called according to his purpose for them." When God causes things to work together for good, it is specifically for the good of **those who love God and are called according to His purpose.** And what is the purpose we are called to? Romans 8:29a, "For God knew his people in advance, and he chose them to become like his Son". God's ultimate purpose for those who love Him is to make them more like Jesus. Every good thing that God gives is meant to grow us, draw us closer to Him, and help us live out the plans He has for us. For every one of us, this will look different in our circumstances. The good outcomes that I listed might not be the same ones you see in your own life. Remarriage or writing your story in a book may not be in your future, but God will bring about good things that are tailored to what you need and what is in line with His best plans for you.

There is one particular "good" that is guaranteed for every person in any situation: the presence and the help of God. Each and every day, we have access to the gifts of His grace, His peace, His love, His joy, His wisdom, His hope, and His strength–freely available to us. We also have the blessing and the promise of His continual presence. All we have to do to receive such gifts is draw near to Him.

At the time of my divorce, it was the hardest, most painful experience of my life. Few things could have flipped my world like it did. But in that pain and brokenness, I drew nearer to God. My initial prayers revolved around the desires and expectations I had for the situation. As time went on, those desires and expectations never came to pass. And I was okay with it! The more time I spent with God, the more my desires shifted, and the more content I was with whatever outcome came from the situation. Would I ever be able to move on, or would this pain wound me forever? Either way, I had God's strength. Would I ever get remarried, or would I stay single? In either scenario, God's love was enough. He gave me peace and a joy that one would never expect to have in such a painful season of life, and it taught me this valuable lesson: There is no suffering that can take away our access to God, and there is no good outcome that supersedes His presence with us.

Even if we have nothing else good in life, we still have God, who will never reject us, will never walk away, and will never find a reason to stop loving us (Romans 8:35-39). We have to ask ourselves: isn't that good enough? Or, to rephrase it, isn't that enough "good"? Because truthfully, the love, joy, and safety that any marriage once offered us is only a shadow of what we can receive from God at all times. To me, that is more than enough good.

"Taste and see that the Lord is good. Oh, the joys of those who take refuge in him! Fear the Lord, you his godly people, for those who fear him will have all they need. Even strong young lions sometimes go hungry, but those who trust in the Lord will lack no good thing." (Psalm 34:8-10, NLT)

A New Perspective

So, are you ready for this new life post-divorce? A life that can be filled with hope, joy, and peace again. Then it's time to see your brokenness from a new perspective.

Romans 8:28 gives us that perspective shift we need. We see God's capacity to carry out His plans for good in spite of the sorrows we endure. He takes the divorce that broke us and uses it to produce good in our lives and in the lives of others; ultimately so that His people and His Kingdom can flourish. And while we might not always be given the good outcomes we want, God always brings about what is best.

The human perspective of suffering is that it leaves us *wholly* broken. A complete, irreparable destruction of our lives leading to despair, fear, and doubt. But from God's perspective, suffering can bring about a *holy* brokenness that leads to new life and new purpose. To be holy in Scripture means to be set apart, and one of the ways we are made holy by God is by being set apart for purposes beyond ourselves. God used my story to lead me here, to serve the purpose of bringing you comfort and insight. If you give God the opportunity, He can use your story to fulfill life-changing purposes as well.

How good is our God, that He restores our broken hearts while He takes the very worst moments of our lives and uses them for greater purposes! And this is why we can embrace every opportunity to thrive in situations we never dreamed we would have to experience.

Next Steps

THINK – What are some of the good things you want to see happen as you navigate life after divorce? What, in your opinion, could God do in your situation to make it better? How disappointed would you be if you didn't receive those things? Is it possible that God could actually have something better in store? Do you trust God to give you what is best?

ASK – Pray this prayer, "God, will you please give me a new perspective on this pain and brokenness I feel? I know that the Bible says you can use it for good, but I'm having a hard time seeing what that good can be. Show me how you can use this brokenness to make me holy and use this divorce for something, or someone's, good. Lead me into a deeper relationship with you and give me wisdom for all the days ahead."

BREATHE – Take a deep breath and take this post-divorce life one day at a time. It will be overwhelming in the beginning, but keep going. One foot in front of the other, one prayer after another, day after day. Let God carry your burdens and trust Him with the process of healing your heart. Don't give up, there is always hope with each new day.

Chapter 10

Trust Fall: Trusting God That I Am Not Alone

By Terra Richards

TRUST IN THE LORD WITH ALL YOUR HEART
AND LEAN NOT ON YOUR OWN UNDERSTANDING
IN ALL YOUR WAYS SUBMIT TO HIM
AND HE WILL MAKE YOUR PATHS STRAIGHT.

PROVERBS 3:5-6 (NIV)

No one gets married expecting to get divorced. I certainly didn't when my Dad walked me down to the lake to meet my incredibly handsome groom on a beautiful day in June. For the next twenty-five years, I put my heart and soul into being my husband's helpmate, a mama of two amazing human beings, and created a business with my husband that was built on a purpose from God. I was living a life I didn't know to dream of and thanked God every day.

When things began to unravel, I held on more tightly to my marriage than I did God because I didn't want to lose my built-in best friend. I was fearful of being all alone. Even when the time together wasn't always pleasant, it seemed better than the alternative of starting over. Yet, unfortunately, we all find ourselves in places that we didn't choose. We are left to evaluate how we ended up here, what we might do differently, and sometimes, we get stuck on who is to blame. But we don't have to stay here.

First, let me say that whether you are reading this for yourself or to support someone you love, I am truly sorry. I understand how difficult this season can be, and I see you. If we were together, I would hug you tightly and promise you, God is with you. You are not alone.

I hope you can find a little humor in one of my favorite quotes by Flannery O'Connor, an American novelist and short story writer in the early 1900s. She states: "I can, with one eye squinted, take it all as a blessing."[7] I have found this to be true in my journey. We can let our unexpected hardships define us or make us stronger. The mere fact that you're holding this book tells me that you are seeking ways to be the latter.

If I could make a suggestion to someone contemplating filing for divorce, do not do it in the winter. It's dark, and unless you live in Hawaii or Florida, it's also cold, and that makes for an increased amount of sadness, and for me, it was fertile ground for intense loneliness. I would definitely choose summer if I had it to do again because of the longer days, sunlight, and the ability to go outside. Yet, God, being smarter than I, knew that if it were summer, I would go and do, never choosing to sit at his feet and worship during this unexpected season of pruning my life.

---

7   Flannery O'Connor, *The Habit of Being: Letters of Flannery O'Connor*, edited by Sally Fitzgerald, Farrar, Straus and Giroux, 1979, p. 100.

Remember the story of Martha and Mary when Jesus came to visit? Jesus came to their home in Bethany, a village near Jerusalem, to teach and share stories. While Jesus is teaching, Mary is sitting at his feet listening intently (Luke 10:38-42). All the while, Martha is getting frustrated because she is frantically running around making preparations. She finally gets frustrated and tattles on Mary to Jesus and asks him to make her help. Who hasn't wanted to do that before? Even as adults, we think, "Lord, look at what they are getting away with. Do you even see their sin?" All the while, we have our own stuff we are dealing with, but we are filled with religious activity, trying to avoid sitting with Jesus to ask what he actually wants us to do.

Jesus responds to Martha, assuring her that Mary has chosen the path to Jesus that can not be taken from her, one to sit and listen. Yet, during a hard season, I found this very difficult to do. Going through a divorce meant sitting alone, a lot. The last thing I wanted to do was be alone, yet this seemed to be what God was calling me to do. Sit still. You know the famous scripture that has been cross-stitched on pillows, as well as craftily painted on repurposed pallets, "Be still, and know that I am God." This is found in Psalm 46:10 NIV, yet somehow the second part of the verse is often left off. The full verse reads "Be still, and know that I am God, I will be exalted among the nations, I will be exalted in the earth." Oh, you mean, I am not just to sit and wallow, but exalt the Lord while I wait?

The definition of exalt is to glorify or praise. So, what I am hearing is that when we are called to "be still and know," we are actually called to praise the Lord. I will be honest. This was really, really hard during a season when I was begging God to heal my marriage, bring my husband home, and wrap it all up in a pretty story where we could use our hardships to inspire those struggling in their own marriages. Yet, this wasn't the story God had for me.

One night after a ton of prayer, devouring devotional books, and probably some whining, I set everything down on the table in front of me. I said out loud, "God, I want to trust you to take care of me in this situation, but I am scared." This is when I got the idea to do a trust fall. I wanted to fall into His arms and trust that he would walk with me through this storm and not abandon me. . I closed my eyes and visualized falling backwards into his arms. Here I am, Lord. I am yours.

Once I decided to fully surrender to God, He rescued me from my pit of pity and began to answer my prayers regarding loneliness. Have you been there? Life knocked you down, and you didn't want to get back up? Divorce can leave us full of fear of the future and feeling very alone. How will I have the picture of life I envisioned again? How will I survive financially on my own? How do I file for divorce, sell my house, support my kids, and face my church, friends, family, and community? How God, how? None of us likes to feel like we are not in control, even though actually being in control is an illusion. So, I might have repeated the trust fall a few times before I actually felt him catch me. I then sat on my knees and praised Him, and asked him for help to not feel so lonely.

My prayer was answered, but not in the way I would have expected. He asked me to start taking steps to create community and bring people into my life. God asked me to host a life group at my house. That is correct. I didn't go tuck away in the back of a support group of women. Instead, I opened my home to sixteen women in all walks of life to join me in an eight-week study my church was doing in January. Yes, it was still dark and cold, but when you know you have sixteen strangers coming for dessert and to talk about purpose, you take off your pajamas, clean the house, and arrange the living room to welcome friends.

Tony Robbins, a well-known thought leader, teaches a concept that when life gets hard, turn outward instead of inward. He says serving others, ultimately, will lead you to feel better yourself. It was amazing to see God weave the details, too, because our church was studying purpose. When leading a life group, you are asked to write a bio of the people you intend to gather with. I wrote, "You were created on purpose for a purpose, so join with women of all ages to serve and learn how to find your purpose in your exact season of life." This created a community of women from twenty-five to sixty-five who were married, separated, and divorced, with little kids at home to college-aged.

This variety of life stages was instrumental in helping me see past my own hurts and focus on others. It was the perfect opportunity for all of us to serve each other, as we each had experience to give and gain from each other. I love that we were able to pray for each other and support one another, and find encouragement in knowing that "Where two or three gather in my name, there I am with them." Matthew 18:20 NIV

Just as when God asked me to be still, but worship him, he brought me community, but I had to do some of the work.

This was an opportunity to show up for others, yet I ended up showing up for myself. He brought me community, but I had to provide the opportunity for it to happen.

When you find yourself going through a divorce, it's easy to pull away from everyone. The last thing you want to do is show up to your normal group of friends and listen to everything they are doing while you feel like you can barely brush your teeth. Yet, this is where God called me to be the most vulnerable. I am a member of a small mastermind group that meets monthly to discuss our personal growth strategies as business leaders, in our families, and personally. It is a high-functioning group of people who push each other to show up in the world as their best selves.

When you find yourself in a pity pit, the last thing that feels good is to be pushed. Yet, on a dark day in January, when I found myself barely able to get out of bed and lacking the desire to eat, the group pushed me. I hated it. I wanted to quit the group and keep feeling sorry for myself. I tried to hide in the calls, the members taking turns sharing "thorns and roses" of what was happening, and my face was in the Zoom lineup. This particular January call, I explained how I was struggling to eat. I had lost a ton of weight, and woe is me. I explained that I couldn't seem to find my way forward in this season. Everyone listened, provided encouragement, and moved on to the next person in the group. I was relieved when the call ended until I heard my phone ring.

It was one of the people in my group calling to give me some tough love. He said I had adopted a victim mentality, and I needed to remember I still had a family I needed to show up for. As I whined about how I just could not eat, my friend coached me, "You can eat, you are choosing not to." Ouch. That afternoon, I drove to a fast food place I rarely frequented just to get calories in my body. I purchased a burger, fries, and even a soda, and began a journey forward knowing I had a community around me that wouldn't let me stay in the pity pit. Even though I was eating food I wouldn't normally choose, I am reminded of the verse "As iron sharpens iron, so one person sharpens another." Proverbs 27:17 NIV. It is good to surround yourself with a variety of people, but the ones who will push you to keep showing up and give tough love are good friends who won't leave your side.

To this point, I had created my own community through hosting the Bible Study, and I had shown up to my community through friendships I had created long before going through a divorce. But the way I saw God move the most was when he showed me I wasn't alone was through specific people. I would pray for very specific things, and God would send people in the airport, at the grocery store, and on my social media feed that had the skills or support I needed, very specific to my needs. Over and over, divine connections like this took place. I would pray, "God, I need help figuring out how to fix a broken sprinkler head," and I would get a text from someone I hadn't talked to in a while to say hello, and I would remember they knew how to help.

I just had to ask, and God provided what I needed exactly when because His timing is perfect. This was also a lesson in humility for me to fully depend on God and ask. Scriptures assure us, "If you believe, you will receive whatever you ask for in prayer." Matthew 21:22 NIV This was a true test of my faith in God for me, would I be able to ask God and then trust that He would provide the community necessary.

It's interesting to think of God as a community, but he is with us, three in one: God the Father, Jesus sitting at God's right hand, and the Holy Spirit in us. When I chose to do a trust fall on a dark, dreary day in January, my first community that surrounded me was the trinity. As I fell into their arms, believing they would catch me, I felt a peace that surpasses understanding, and I found confidence knowing I could lean in during the hurting season and my heart and mind would be guarded as we are told in scripture in Philippians 4:7 NIV. The peace definitely came from knowing my heart and mind would be guarded. I can't say I didn't still have fear of the future and all the what-ifs I mentioned earlier, but as I leaned into this community, I also leaned into scripture and reading. I leaned on scriptures like "For God has not given [me] a spirit of fear but of power and of love and of a sound mind" in 2 Timothy 1:7 (NKJV) because I was still so fearful. However, as I continued to press into Jesus and find scriptures to combat my mind, praise Him while I sat still in obedience, God daily began to show up and help me continue to build a community of people where I felt supported.

My prayer for you as you walk through this unexpected, seemingly unfair season is that you can trustfall into Jesus' arms, too. I know it sounds a little weird, but try it first with a friend or on your couch. Stand up, close your eyes, and pray, "God, I trust you to carry me through this season." You can also pray Romans 8:28 (NIV): "And we know that in all things God works for the good of those who love him." Commit to love Jesus with all your heart, close your eyes, and fall back into his love, mercy, and goodness, knowing this truth, that all things work for good. He loves you, he sees you, and not one tear drop will go unseen by God. So, trust him with all your heart, don't try to see to the end, just feel his arms wrap all the way around you and raise your hands to praise him, then be prepared to see the miracle of a beautiful community of the most surprising people will create a tapestry that you can walk forward with and feel it wrapped around your shoulders keeping you safe and warm.

Next Steps

Carve out quiet time in a special place you like to meet with the Lord. Put on some worship music and sit at the feet of Jesus, and acknowledge your full trust in Him. Spend time in worship and reading scripture, asking for a specific verse that will lead you to put your trust fully in him to be all you need. Maybe try a trust fall of your own.

Seek out opportunities to serve others. Turning your focus outward will help you to ease your pain by supporting others in their pain. You will be surprised at how joy will fill your heart, and you will forget all about your own troubles for a little while. You might even meet a new friend.

Ask a trusted group of friends to hold you accountable. Whether you need to begin exercising, eating, or just getting off Netflix, it's good to create a group of even just a couple of friends who will ask you every day if you are keeping the promises you made to yourself.

Pray very specific prayers when you need people in your life to help you. It tells us in Matthew 7:7, if we ask, it will be given to us. Pray this specifically! "God, you say in your word that if I ask, it will be given to me. I trust you. I need someone to help me get my kids to practice tomorrow." Then, believe that he will show up!

About the Authors

Bridget Gengler

Bridget Gengler has been an elementary educator for over 25 years. Her love of writing is deeply connected to her passion for nurturing young minds. She finds great joy in witnessing the spark that ignites in her students as they grow into confident readers and writers. Bridget is the published author of the children's book "*Hold Your Head Up and Walk with Grace*". She has two more children's books scheduled for release in the summer and fall of 2025. Bridget currently lives in Southern California with her husband and their blended family of young adult children.

Connect with Bridget:
www.bridgetgengler.com
Facebook: https://www.facebook.com/Blessedwithagratefulheart
Facebook: https://www.facebook.com/bridget.gengler
Instagram: https://www.instagram.com/BridgetGengler

About the Authors

Julie Smith

*J*ulie Wilson Smith has faced many challenges. She believed that marriage was for a lifetime. When it became evident that it was not going to be she committed herself to raising her four children alone with help from family. Her writing is a way to encourage others and showcase how God is working even in difficult situations. Today she spends time with her family and friends. She has 4 adult children and 11 grandchildren. Her main desire in writing is to encourage others with her story and how her faith in God was the single most important part of her survival.

Connect with Julie:

Facebook: https://www.facebook.com/julie.smith.775853/
Instagram: https://www.instagram.com/julie.w.smith

Jennifer Burchill

Jennifer is the author of *Gifts of Gratitude*, a heartfelt collection that blends Midwest memories with reflections on appreciation, connection, and legacy. She is on a mission to help others express gratitude to those who've made a difference—right here and now. Fascinated by people's stories, Jennifer believes everyone has a story worth sharing. Her writing—and her work as a technical program manager—are grounded in a belief that small acts of appreciation can create lasting impact, both personally and professionally. She loves traveling, reading, crossing off Bucket List items and going to concerts with her son and daughter.

Connect with Jennifer:

https://jenniferburchill.com/

Facebook: https://www.facebook.com/jennifer.burchill.author

Instagram: https://www.instagram.com/jennifer_burchill

About the Authors

Takhia Gaither

Takhia Gaither, CEO/Founder of The Ready Write-Her Writing Services, is an international speaker, multi-time Amazon Bestselling author, editor, author/co-author of over 20 books, and creator of various journals and planners. As an accomplished mathematics, technology, and computer science teacher with over 20 years of experience in urban school districts, she also uses her expertise and teaching skills as a freelance curriculum developer and writing coach. A mother of two and native of Baltimore, MD, Takhia holds degrees in Teacher Education (AA), Mathematics (BS), and Information Technology (MS). She is currently pursuing her PhD in Christian Education.

Connect with Takhia:
Website: https://www.thereadywriteher.com/
Facebook: https://www.facebook.com/takhiatheteacher
Instagram: https://www.instagram.com/takhiatheteacher
LinkedIn: https://www.linkedin.com/in/takhia-gaither/
TikTok: https://www.tiktok.com/@takhiatheteacher

Amy L. Boyd

Amy Boyd is a writer and certified Go and Tell Gals coach with a heart for Christian women facing the pain and complexity of divorce. Her work has been featured in *Truly Magazine* and *For Every Mom*, offering honest, faith-filled encouragement. By day, she teaches reading; by night, she's chasing her curious wire fox terrier around their Michigan home. The Great Lakes bring her peace, and she never says no to a rosemary latte and a good book.

Connect with Amy:

https://www.revivemeagain.com/

Instagram: https://www.instagram.com/amyboydwrites/

Substack: https://substack.com/@amylboyd?utm_source=user-menu

About the Authors

Angela King Bley

Angela Bley is an ordained minister at Abba's House in Hixson, Tennessee. Angela loves encouraging couples and helping them see that a strong, joy-filled marriage really is possible. She and Tom have walked through their own journey of healing and restoration, and they've seen firsthand how powerful God's Word can be when it's lived out. Thanks to God's amazing grace, their lives and marriage have been redeemed and renewed. For over 18 years, He's continued to fill them with hope, and it all started with a few small, faithful steps forward.

She and her husband, Tom, live in Ooltewah, Tennessee and have been married for over 18 years. They have a wonderful, blended family of four kids and their spouses, nine grandkids, and even a great-grandchild!

Connect with Angela:

hopeineveryseason.org
Email: angelabley1@gmail.com
Facebook: https://www.facebook.com/AngelaDBley
Instagram: https://www.instagram.com/tenngirl0365

Amber Brandt

Amber Brandt is a StoryBrand certified freelance copywriter and The Coziness Consultant, an interior decorator. She is passionate about helping clients and families create spaces that not only reflect their values, but help them live smarter, cozier, and more intentional lives. She believes authenticity, connection, and true hospitality can change the world. Amber lives in Grand Rapids, Michigan with her husband Kyle and daughter/fairy Winslow, and has been featured in a variety of outlets including Better Homes & Gardens, Apartment Therapy, and Parade Magazine. She writes and speaks about faith, family, values-based living, and all things cozy.

Connect with Amber:

Website: thecozinessconsultant.com

Facebook: facebook.com/thecozinessconsultant

Instagram: instagram.com/thecozinessconsultant

Substack: https://amberbrandt.substack.com/

About the Authors

Ashley Boswell

With over twenty-five years of experience as a Christian Counselor and drawing from her own journey of overcoming relationship trauma, she founded the Unbridled Faith Program to support women in their healing process. She deeply understands the pain of relationship trauma, further evidenced by her work as the Founder of Shepherd Youth Ranch, a non-profit providing equine-assisted therapy to over 1,000 trauma survivors annually. Through this work, she has witnessed firsthand Christ's transformative power to heal both body and mind. Her passion for empowering women to heal, grow in their faith, and discover their God-given potential is a driving force in her life.

Connect with Ashley:
www.unbridledfaithbox.com
Facebook: http://facebook.com/unbridledfaith
Instagram: https://www.instagram.com/ashleyeboswell

Stephanie Lauren Jordan

Stephanie Jordan is a Christian writer and speaker who has a heart for helping the poor in spirit find hope and healing. She is an active member of her local church and an advocate for better mental health resources within the global church. In her free time she enjoys the simpler things in life: reading, puzzles, walks and bike rides, and sharing a good meal with loved ones. Stephanie lives in Orlando, FL with her husband, James.

Connect with Stephanie:
https://slaurenjordan.com/
Instagram: https://www.instagram.com/slaurenjordan

About the Authors

Terra Richards

Terra Richards is a visionary in intentional living, helping people cultivate growth inside and out. With over 37 years studying personal development and 20 years as an entrepreneur and marketing expert she authentically shares her inspiration and expertise in: health, nature inspired home design, business, and faith. She is the CEO of Stump Plants where she offers nature inspired goods, as well as a curated selection of books for personal growth. Terra lives in Fort Worth, Texas with her son and white Labrador Olive. She also has a daughter attending Savannah College of Art and Design.

Connect with Terra:
Facebook: https://www.facebook.com/terra.n.richards
Facebook: https://www.facebook.com/FossilCreekTreeFarm
Instagram: https://www.instagram.com/terrarichardswrites/
Instagram: https://www.instagram.com/thehaven.est2015/

Closing

Dear Reader,

Thank you for reading *Rediscovering You: A Guide to Life After Divorce!*

I want to take a moment to celebrate the incredible authors who contributed to this meaningful book. They have poured their hearts into discovering, clarifying, and sharing their unique messages—and now, you get to benefit from their hard work and dedication.

At hope*books, we are deeply proud of our authors and are honored to partner with them on this journey. If you've ever considered writing and publishing your book, we invite you to visit hopebooks.com to learn more about our coaching and publishing services. We believe that everyone has a message to share and an audience to serve, and the world needs your hopeful words now more than ever.

Once again, let's take a moment to celebrate the hard work of these authors in bringing *Rediscovering You* to life.

Sincerely,

Brian Dixon

Publisher, hope*books

Looking to *connect* with a community of writers?

hope✱writers
www.hopewriters.com

The world needs your *hope-filled* words more now than ever before.

Thinking about *writing* your own book?

hope✱books
www.hopebooks.com

Made in the USA
Columbia, SC
13 June 2025

ffe02c81-82ef-47f4-a8e9-809852742e3fR01